CRIME STOPPERS

By the same author:
Kiss Ma Bell Good-bye: How to Install Your Own Telephones, Extensions & Accessories

CRIME STOPPERS

Low-Cost,* No-Cost Ways to Protect Yourself, Your Family, Your Home, and Your Car

WESLEY COX

Illustrated with drawings by Bruce T. Miyake

*For under $10

CROWN PUBLISHERS, INC.   NEW YORK

This book is dedicated to the memory of Howard Messler, Jr., of Trenton and all other communities in New Jersey where he was known and loved by everyone who had the privilege of his company. Howard was almost sixty years of age when he was adopted into our family group. He then proceeded to show us the truths in nature, the flaws in many things we do, the skills we so often neglect, and the best ways of getting through each day without hurting ourselves or other living things.

Grateful acknowledgment is given to *US News & World Report* for their permission to reprint material from the November 1, 1982, issue.

Published by Crown Publishers, Inc., One Park Avenue, New York, New York 10016, and simultaneously in Canada by General Publishing Company Limited

Printed in the United States of America

Library of Congress Cataloging in Publication Data

Cox, Wesley.
  Crime stoppers.

  Includes index.
  1. Crime prevention. 2. Dwellings—Security measures. I. Title.
HV7431.C67 1983   643'.16   83-6639
ISBN 0-517-55102-0
10 9 8 7 6 5 4 3 2 1
First Edition

CONTENTS

ACKNOWLEDGMENTS

In addition to the doctor and Harry who provoked the author relentlessly even while assisting him intermittently, there were mentors, experts, and authorities who provided the skills and opinions that made this book a reality.

L. Stephen Pleasant worked hardest of all providing art assistance to illustrator Bruce T. Miyake. In addition to names and identities mentioned within the text, there were significant contributions by F. E. Smith, Gordon Stewart, Gerard Weber, Cullen Schippe, Harry Sternberg, L. and N. Serene, Ginny Doscher, and the late T. Spencer Meyer, each of whom provided an idea, a unique skill or concept to aid this project.

The special agents of the Klinger and Kohner Protection Services, who insist on remaining anonymous, may at least be recognized in this space for valuable assistance and advice along the way.

The author is indebted to the Bart family who, with David James and Gary Douglas, kept *Crime Stoppers* on track even when excursions into other areas seemed more attractive to the writer.

The bottom line, however, is the certain fact that the professional staff of Crown Publishers—in particular, the team working with Editor Lisa Healy—made the whole thing possible and coherent and enjoyable. Because of their skillful and tender, loving care, the book may prove to be a thing of value to those most important individuals of all, our readers.

1

EIGHT MILLION CRIMINALS

Have you ever awakened in panic that a stranger was invading your residence?

Have you ever experienced the bewilderment of going to get your car only to find it missing? Then the shock of disbelief that someone has stolen it? Have you felt violated?

Have you ever returned to your home or office to find it ransacked, your possessions ripped away, your living space despoiled, ravaged?

Have you known the fear of finding yourself in a dark or alien location, suddenly shaken with apprehension that you might be assaulted in the very next second?

These have become commonplace events and reactions in today's society.

WE CAN BEAT THE BAD GUYS

Most of us have convinced ourselves it won't happen to us. We mumble to ourselves about crime prevention and getting involved. All too often our good intentions are defeated by the press of other matters, or a shortage of funds, or an uncertainty about how to get started. This book will describe and illustrate devices, techniques, and inner attitudes that can thwart any attacks on our persons or property. In most cases the devices can be homemade and installed without a penny of cost. Others will cost a few dollars. A few will reach or exceed the arbitrary limit of $10 that I set when I began to develop this compendium.

If a person is willing to invest a bit of time, these low-cost and no-cost things will be manageable by novice do-it-yourselfers. Yet the devices themselves, when installed, will perform as well as, or maybe better than, store-bought gadgets costing hundreds, even thousands, of dollars.

In this book you'll find references to many of these superrich things, too. If you don't have the time or inclination to do things yourself, you'll find a directory of people and places to provide any kind of security your heart desires and a big, fat bankroll can afford. All of that expensive stuff is pushed to the back end of the book, mostly Chapter 10. By the time you get there you'll have a reasonably good idea of what's available and how to get started.

DON'T SKIP THE BASICS

Although the concept of this book is low-cost and no-cost security, there's no requirement that you have to get your hands dirty doing it yourself. Sure, there are dozens of protection devices that you can devise, invent, find, rig up, and otherwise create for free all by yourself. Maybe you'd rather pay the bright young high-school kid down the street a few dollars to do it for you. That's okay. No matter what your objective, the means will be described in this book. The one important thing, the overall, ultimate, for-Pete's-sake-stop-kidding-yourself thing, is to *do something* to protect yourself, your loved ones, and your possessions.

One of the several experts in crime prevention who read through this book in manuscript declared, "If ninety percent of your readers would do five percent of the things you advocate in this book, then virtually one hundred percent of criminal activity would be wiped out within a year." That's a very nice compliment.

But compliments won't keep you from being mugged, ripped off, or murdered if you simply skim through the book, look at the pretty pictures, and park the whole thing behind the birdcage. Let's keep two simple objectives in mind. First, let's see what we can do to protect ourselves and our possessions either free, at modest cost, or by paying a pro to do it for us. Meanwhile, as a secondary goal, let's do what we can to make criminal activity a nonprofit business.

Let me put some important words on your lips: "Who, me? How can I keep from being victimized in today's crummy society? How can I defend myself? And who's out to get me, anyway?" Here's news: There are 8 million creeps in this part of the hemisphere who would think little if anything about knocking you down, stealing your possessions, or doing personal, violent, obscene things to you. So what should we do about it?

Increasingly in the 1980s, the cry is being heard, "Stop 'em. Lock 'em up and throw the keys away." Yet we all know there's not sufficient room to warehouse the criminals we've already got on our hands. *US News & World Report* commented (November 1, 1982), "Justices are handing out stiffer jail terms these days, but that is no panacea: Prisons are already overflowing, and there is no relief in sight."

Taxpayers are demanding that governmental budgets be cut, not expanded. Major metropolitan police forces are being reduced. In 1983 several communities actually went bankrupt, even after shutting down vital services such as police departments the previous year.

Based on the known facts of four hundred thousand inmates in jails right now, with eight million criminals on the loose, it's simple arithmetic that we'd need twenty times the number of jail cells we now have if it were possible to capture and imprison all the major offenders in our society.

Inevitably, therefore, one must conclude that each person would be prudent to take some appropriate legal and practical steps to reinforce his or her own personal security and the protection of loved ones and personal property. Vigilance without vigilantes, okay?

2

WHERE ARE WE GOING? HOW DO WE GET THERE?

Our destination, to achieve personal, family, home, property, and community security can be reached by anyone willing to expend a bit of effort.

GOING FOR SECURITY

The precise route and the specific target cannot be laid out one, two, three, because there are so many variables—the areas where we live, the types of criminals who work in our neighborhoods, and a grand hodgepodge of other differences. The opening moves in the game are easy to describe. You take a bit of this, some of that, and a few of those, and pretty soon you've got yourself a working system.

For starters, we'll be discussing the use of broomsticks, nails, wire scraps, plastic foil, 10-cent switches, free batteries, broken telephones, bent rods, clothespins, and string for devices that can keep criminals away from our homes, our businesses, and our bodies.

Then we'll venture into homemade annunciators that can be built for pennies or a few dollars, depending on your curiosity and the contents of a junk box. And don't let that word *annunciator* scare you. An annunciator is simply the board, box, or clump in which a few alarm components are brought together. If you're ever in doubt about any of the words that crop up, glance at the glossary beginning on page 142. In no time at all you'll sound like an expert.

THE REALISTIC OBJECTIVE

Now hear this. Then forget it. We have to accept the bad news that we'll simply never be able to assure ourselves of 100 percent security, guaranteed forever. Tragic events of recent times have proved that even a pope and a president of the United States can become targets of assassins' madness.

At this point I can tell you that nowhere in this book will you find my advocacy of anything related to firearms as protective devices for me or you or our loved ones. Personally, I think that guns, whether handguns, rifles, shotguns, or any other form of explosive weaponry, are dangerous to have around. If you love your firearms, I wish you good luck with them, and remind you that each year more than two thousand innocent gun owners, children, bystanders, and just plain folks are killed outright and thousands more are wounded accidentally. There may well be certain types of hunters and security personnel whose pastimes, work, and personal safety necessarily involve firearms. But as for others, if I can convince them, somehow, that a clothespin switch or cactus plant makes a much more effective security device, we'll all be better off and better protected.

Anyone who leads a reasonable life in a recognizably respectable neighborhood should be able to achieve a high level—say, 99 percent attainment—of reliable security. The first and essential component is a keen interest in the subject of self-protection. The rest of the process seems to fall into line, piece by piece, logically, without stress, at whatever out-of-pocket cost one wishes to invest and can afford.

LOTS OF VARIABLES

Without exception, the sizable number of police, security consultants, and other specialists I quizzed in writing this book all agree there's no single security system to accommodate every situation.

Furthermore, areas are different, sometimes within a few blocks, in the types of criminals who operate within them. For example, statistics reveal that in the oceanside community where I reside, 95 percent of the criminals must be classified as amateurs, half of whom are juveniles. Fewer than five in a hundred would have the vaguest idea about picking locks, holding up a bank, or "casing a mark"—that is, carefully planning a crime in the manner of a professional burglar.

A few miles away, farther east, in the Beverly Hills–Bel Air sections, the true professionals outnumber the amateurs three to one. These are the rascals who know the inner workings of every alarm and most installations. There are specialists among them: types who can bug phone lines and divert silent alarms, others who can pop the combinations on heavy-duty safes, and even couriers who deal with domestic servants to learn the movements of homeowners and clear the way for burglaries.

The ways of midwestern criminals differ from that of southerners. New Yorkers are confronted with an entirely different set of burglary modes. For example, the fire escapes in New York City, the air shafts, and the rooftop configurations present conditions for theft and assault quite unlike those to be found in Boston or Baltimore.

However, this book attempts to present such a variety of techniques that you'll find devices and methods that are most practical not only for your area and your bankbook, but also for your skills at doing things yourself.

And here's the best part—and it's really the most important part.

If you can customize your security system, you'll be miles ahead of everyone else. Throughout this whole adventure, keep your thoughts tuned to setting up security systems and attitudes that will catch any would-be attacker completely offguard. Confront the criminal with a gadget, a situation, a device that in combination with other things might be utterly unlike anything he (or she) has seen before. Instantly, if not sooner, your would-be bad guy will leave your territory and go look for a residence, office, or individual who looks like an easier, more routine rip-off.

In 1972 I lived in a courtyard townhouse complex in Beverly Hills, on Palm Drive between Santa Monica Boulevard and Beverly Boulevard. One evening, when all four families on our side of the court were away from home, a pair or trio of burglars broke into the residences adjoining mine. My good, dear neighbors were cleaned out of every valuable, and some of their most precious belongings, such as photos and documents, were destroyed. Feces were smeared on beautiful sofas. Tables were toppled, drawers ripped open, their contents smashed and vandalized. All four of our residences were double-latched, and metal signs near each door identified the burglar system that was installed. The wiring to the alarm bells on all four of the systems had been deactivated, and entry had been made through rear-patio French doors. Of the four residences, mine was the only one that was not vandalized, though it was flanked on both sides by victimized places. Why? We can only guess. But my residence, unlike the others, had a couple of features going for it. I'd taped all front and rear windows decoratively with photographic foil (as described on p. 60), and three miniature LED flashing red lights (see p. 80) had been positioned in the lower corners of the three most vulnerable window areas.

My investment for foil had been less than $5, for the lights and batteries not more than $1.50 each at that time. And they were nothing but passive, unconnected, cosmetic deterrents that I'd installed in an hour or two when we first moved in, a year earlier.

But most likely, according to the supersharp detectives and other police officers in Beverly Hills, my little toy gadgets had been enough to cause the burglary artists to keep moving away from my place. Less than $10 worth of miscellaneous things had done a better job of protecting our property than the $2,000 combination silent and would-be-noisy alarm system.

"You ought to write a book about this thing someday," said my wife. Here, at last, is the book that sprang from that unexpected beginning.

IT TAKES ALL KINDS

In the neighborhood where we now reside, there are three of us who hang out together whenever there's an opportunity to share a few hours. Before and during our ever-deepening friendship we were adding security to our homes. I'd moved into this area at almost the same time that a rash of ugly criminal activity had broken out, including the first whole-family homicide ever recorded in this small city.

The doctor's place, next to mine, has been outfitted professionally with three independent, redundant burglar/fire alarm systems. I know only too well, because one or more of them frequently cuts loose with false alarms. The doctor, who helped goad me into this book, figures that in the past fifteen years he's handed out more than $20,000 for the various installations, updates, and their maintenance.

Harry, our salesman pal on the next block, is an electronics freak. He built up his own security system mostly from junk in his scrap box plus a few items from the specialty shops that thrive in this part of the country, mostly in electronics. Take my word that, if nothing else, his security system would cause any intruder to stop breaking and entering just to stand there staring as lights flashed, alarms rang, strobes blasted, and a telephone system announced it was already dialing an alarm service as well as Harry himself on a forwarding circuit. A tape-recorded message would cut in, advising the rogue that his picture has just been taken from three angles and his best bet is to sit on the floor with his hands clasped atop his head until the police arrive to take him for a free ride.

The doctor and I love it. Harry's wife despises it.

"I feel deprived," she said one day. "I haven't got any keys anymore. Look. Just key cards. Plastic. Plus a bunch of numbers I have to remember to punch into the door entries and the car ignition. I feel like I'm a computer already."

Harry has no idea how much money he has invested in all his security gadgetry but guesses it might cost a couple of hundred dollars as junk, a thousand if he wanted to duplicate it at retail.

"Plus all the fun time I've had," he adds, smiling.

My own personal in-house system is mostly passive. I have less than $25 in the whole shebang, although that doesn't count the doodads in the two cars and my wife's super-gee-whiz handbags, (all of which are illustrated elsewhere in this book). My house system is a cosmetic fakery. It couldn't ring a bell, dial a policeman, or even say boo if it were attacked. But, having grown out of the Beverly Hills experience, it's got some five-and-dime-store features that would drive a burglar to drink if only he knew how innocent they are.

You'll get a rundown on all these things plus a few dozen other devices and techniques that the doctor, Harry, and I have checked in and checked out, back and forth, in our ever-changing security show-and-tells.

FUMBLE FINGERS ARE NO EXCUSE

Most folks, when invited to wire a clothespin, chisel a stick, or pound a nail, tend to panic. "I can't do that. I'm not handy with tools."

Nuts! The homemade security systems sketched out for you in this book require only the most klutzy tools, if, indeed, any at all. Hammer and nails will be great. A screwdriver is a big plus. A drill, even the dime-store variety, will be of great assistance. An electric drill—wow!

For some of the electronic and electrical things there'll be reason for a smear of solder here and there. If the thought of a soldering iron boggles you, surely you can get some help from the kid down the street. But really, you can do it yourself if you try.

THE SUPERIORITY OF THE AMATEUR

Unless you're into high explosives or nuclear fission, you can probably do a better job as an amateur than any professional in this business of personal and property security. Amateurs stick at things until they get 'em right. They're working because they want to save time and/or money and/or they have a simple desire for self-satisfaction and accomplishment. Can you think of anything more fulfilling than spending a few hours tightening up your house and then sitting back to enjoy yourself, to lavish praise upon yourself for extraordinary effort in counteracting the bogeyman?

Take my pal the doctor. He readily admits to his self-deception that he really dreamed up his lavish, redundant/redundant security scramble. But it's become his hobby. He's probably fooling around in Harry's basement workshop right at this minute, trying to wire up some kind of infrared add-on. And he's likely wearing surgical gloves, gown, and cap in case he gets a rush call on his beeper phone while he's arguing with Harry about heat-sinking a transistor.

Harry's messing around with an old EKG machine that the doctor picked up. He thinks maybe it'll convert to some other kind of gizmo that'll scare the burglars out of our area.

Good. We need all the help we can get.

Meanwhile, I'll stick to this book to make our know-how available to you. Here's why.

THE TRIPLE PLAY

This year, within six consecutive days, an old friend was mugged, a neighbor had her car stolen from her driveway, and my son was robbed of virtually everything he'd just moved into his new house in Mar Vista, California. After the first shock of hearing the news from each of them I felt a bit angry that they hadn't taken steps to counter such possibilities. Then I realized there were some basic reasons for their shortfalls in security consciousness.

My friend always thought everybody in the world was as kind and honest as he.

The neighbor is, by her own admission, preoccupied, a euphemism for absentminded. She not only forgot to lock her car regularly, she frequently forgot where she'd parked it.

My son is the producer of a television show. He works long and late hours and had not had time to secure things in his new house. And whenever he has some time off he much prefers to play softball.

All three of them did something about security after their personal encounters with criminals. My friend is having a wonderful time taking an innovative self-defense course two evenings each week. Only hours ago he phoned to say he can now face the once-abhorrent thought of breaking an attacker's arm, and furthermore, he would do it if there were no other recourse. My neighbor maintains flashing LEDs (see page 80) on her new dashboard, in her briefcase lock, on her desk, and on her window ledges. They've come to represent brainteasers to her. They remind her to remember, she says.

My son spent $100 of his landlord's money plus $50 of his own to change locks, add timers, and light up his perimeter. He claims that the most important security features in his house are the 40 cents' worth of nails he used to latch up every window and all the door stops.

Why do we wait to be hit before doing things to protect ourselves? Why not zap the crooks before they zap us?

On the pages that follow, the illustrations on the right-hand, odd-numbered pages show devices or techniques outlined on the facing pages. At the beginning of most chapters there is a quick appraisal of things to consider before launching into the subject.

Even if the idea of doing any kind of security project by yourself is a complete turnoff to you, the material will give you basic training in the subject before you traipse off to buy high-technology equipment at fancy installation charges. Although some do-it-yourselfers have whacked a thumb or stubbed a toe in the pursuit of their achievements, nobody, as far as the record shows, has ever been disabled by reading about it.

Let's get started.

3 HOW TO FORTIFY AND SECURE DOORS

On Memorial Day last year I was called by a friend who lives in a house that I know would sell readily for more than a million dollars.

"Would you mind coming over with some tools and helping me patch up the side door from the utility room into the alley? The cat has ripped it to pieces."

The cat? My friend does not harbor a Bengal tiger. I know this fellow's cat personally. It's an everyday, medium-size, curl-up-anywhere-and-fall-asleep tabby. Yet later I saw for myself that Bartholomew, in a fit of pique at being locked in the laundry room, had gone to work on his plastic pet door and then continued to demolish most of the main bottom panel of the section designed for people.

That $1-million house has a $10,000 security system and a hollow-core exterior door that could not possibly have cost more than $4.98 when the house was built, a couple of decades ago. The door is mostly a louvered arrangement with a crank handle and an exterior screen of the type that's interwoven with wires connected to the main alarm. We'll discuss such things in detail later.

BEATING THE SYSTEM

After the cat had wiped out the small plastic pet door he did a number on the surrounding wood. The hollow-core construction depends on a fragile egg crate of lath sandwiched between two ultrathin skins of one-ply veneer, held in place by glue.

The resulting hole was a jagged mess through which a beer

barrel might have rolled without having to inhale. The upper section had not been violated. The screening hadn't been touched. There'd been no alarm. My friend estimated the hole must have been ripped in the door at least forty-eight hours earlier. The bells hadn't rung, the police and detectives at the alarm service hadn't seen any extraordinary activity on their display panel, and for certain the cat hadn't said a word.

If any jockey-size burglar had wandered past the location, he could have had a field day. As things turned out, we simply re-sandwiched the door with hardboard panels, which I also wired into the screen circuit.

How are your doors? Are the exterior doors made of sturdy stuff?

How many movies have you seen where the police officers or crooks simply kick a door open or bash it down with a shoulder slam? Do your doors look like movie material?

Tap them. Top. Middle. Bottom. If they're solid, they'll hurt your knuckles and respond with sounds of strength. If they feel weak and hollow, you'll know it. Get rid of them.

A window set into a door is usually called a *light*. If you have one or more lights in your door, examine the possibility of breaking one of them from the outside, reaching in, and unlocking the latch. And by the way, disregard any old stereotypes you may have seen about picking locks and smashing glass. With the decreasing numbers of real professional crooks there's a sharp decline in those who have the skills to pick locks. They can make a better living as law-abiding locksmiths. And there aren't many glass-smashers in the business nowadays. It makes a lot of noise, and the crook could cut himself on jagged glass. With modern carbide-tip and diamond glass cutters, even the amateurs can zip a circle or square out of a glass window and snap it out quietly with a vacuum cup about as fast as it took you to read this sentence.

It's no big secret among the creeps that one nifty way to break into any location is to tape up a window with masking tape and whap it firmly with the fleshy side of the fist. The glass cracks but doesn't make any falling sounds because it's stuck to the tape.

DOORS—BASIC SECURITY (UNDER $10)

In the illustration (a), opposite, you'll see how hollow-core doors are made—cheaply, without weight, without strength, and often without integrity. Peel off the thin skins and you find—not much! They may be practical for interior closet openings. I, personally, dislike them even for bathroom doors because they succumb readily to moisture and are anything but soundproof.

The door in the center of the page (b) is better, particularly if it's very old, very heavy, and very cheap (secondhand). It'll probably come loaded with good hardware, too, if you find one in a reliable wrecking yard. I prefer the type with decorative molding that has been added rather than hollowed out (routed) by machinery.

My brother-in-law builds his own doors, as shown in illustration (c). Its two exterior door skins are thin and inexpensive (about $3.50 each). A door like this made of tough lumber, reinforcing rods, and cement will finish out within our $10 range. It'll weigh 125 to 150 pounds and may require a mechanical door closer to keep it from slamming through the wall, but it'll be worth it when it's properly fitted. My relative's fundamental door theory is that it should be easier to smash out a wall than knock down its door.

Another way of beefing up a door is to cover it with sheet metal, but the cost can get high and the decoration is something I've never tried and shudder to contemplate. An armoring company will lay sheet metal on a door and cover the metal with door skins. You've got lots of options, eh?

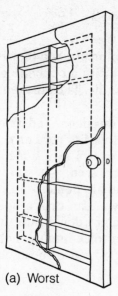

(a) Worst

Simplified
hollow-core door

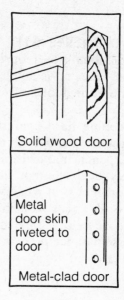

Solid wood door

Metal
door skin
riveted to
door

Metal-clad door

(b) Good

(c) Best

The reinforced-
concrete door

Building the Concrete Door

(1) On a perfectly flat surface, build frame of 2 × 4s and glue to door skin.
(2) Glue scraps of 2 × 4 blocks and add reinforcing rods tied together with wire.
(3) Fill door level with cement.
(4) After three days of drying and curing, smear wood surfaces with adhesive and place top door skin onto door.
(5) Install final door hardware.

2 × 4 frame   Rods and wires   Wood scraps   Window of
2 × 4s

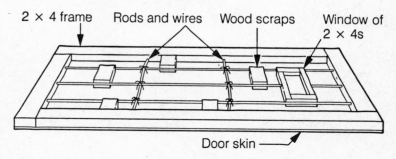

Door skin

STICK TRICK FOR DOORS (FREE–$1)

Broomsticks work sensationally as door reinforcers, and they're usually easy to find, free. One end is notched with a penknife or handsaw to fit snugly under the doorknob spindle. The other end is sawed off square.

Position the stick, pushing hard against the door, and then make a fine pencil mark where the bottom of the stick rests on the floor. Now, leaving the pencil mark visible, chisel a tiny niche into the flooring, barely deep enough to be seen, yet sturdy enough to hold that door tight shut when you are home.

If you have a small drill, about $3/16$ inch, you can drill a hole vertically through the base of the stick, straight down into the floorboard. Drop a coarse nail, ice pick, or nutpick into the hole to make sure the stick can't be wiggle-waggled out of position.

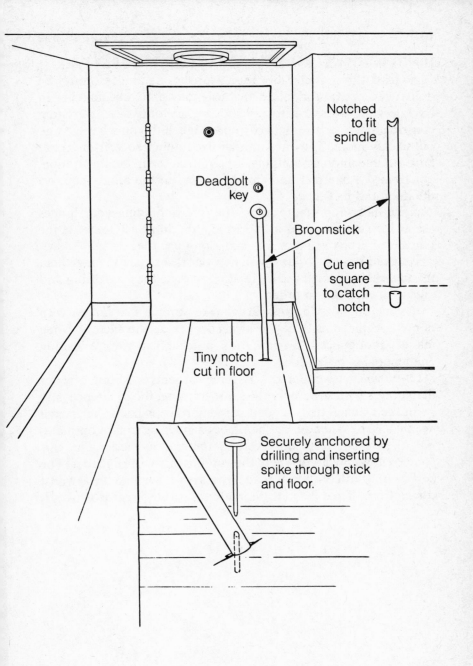

Notched to fit spindle

Deadbolt key

Broomstick

Cut end square to catch notch

Tiny notch cut in floor

Securely anchored by drilling and inserting spike through stick and floor.

HINGES—OFTEN KNOWN AS BUTTS ($1–$4 PER PAIR)

At least three, preferably four, sturdy butt hinges should be used on every exterior door. Obviously they should be matched in thickness and width, so if you're adding one or two to an existing construction, take a sample of your hinge with you when you go out to buy more. They are standardized items, so you shouldn't have trouble finding additional sets. As you see in the illustration, you'll need a hammer and chisel to trim out the hinge space on the door and its frame.

Now, most important, unless the screws holding your hinges are at least an inch and a half in length, don't use them. If the hinge pins aren't as fat as a pencil, don't use them.

Wily old-timers working with new doors set one top hinge first, then mark and install the succeeding ones as they go, fitting and adjusting each one in order.

If your doors swing outward, make sure to use hinges with nonremovable pins. They're swaged over at the factory when made. (Pronounced *swedged,* it's a technical word meaning "hammered oversize.")

If you've ever wondered why some carpenters do much better than others with seemingly the same training, the difference may be in their pencil tips. A good carpenter keeps his or her pencil needle-sharp. When he or she places a ruler or square on material, there's only one thin, certain impression made. The carpenter knows precisely where the cut of a saw will be made. (The kerf is the width of the cut made by a saw. It's where the sawdust comes from. Take it from the material to be discarded, okay?)

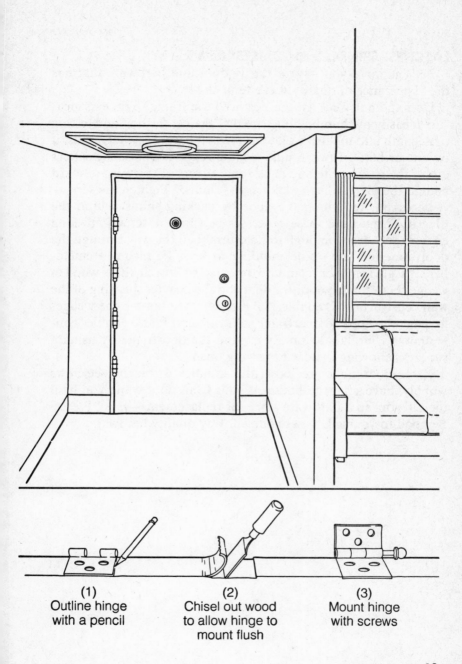

(1)
Outline hinge
with a pencil

(2)
Chisel out wood
to allow hinge to
mount flush

(3)
Mount hinge
with screws

LATCHES, SPINDLES, AND SETSCREWS

Let's suppose you have a sturdy door and hardware that has the appearance of quality. Let's look closer.

Does the bolt click all the way into the frame? You can measure it easily by thumbnailing a pencil against the bolt and testing that length into the strike plate. If the bolt barely catches, adjust it by one or both of two simple techniques. First, back the screws out of the strike plate and pack some slivers of sturdy cardboard behind the plate. They're known as "shims." Tighten the screws. If necessary, reposition the door by packing shims behind the hinges. Throughout these processes be sure the screws are long enough and strong enough to hold firmly all the way through the doorframe into the inside studding, at least 1½ inches. Remember, it's always been standard practice to install little wooden wedges between the door framing and the heavier studding of the wall construction. It enables the carpenters to tap-tap the wedges to make the finished doorframe stand square. It also enables contemporary burglars to simply expand the doorframe by using a car jack, allowing the door to swing open.

If the doorknobs are loose, the spindles worn, the setscrews wobbly, have someone house-sit your front door while you haul the old stuff to a hardware store for replacements—*now!* Please! Be good to yourself. Treat yourself. Buy quality hardware.

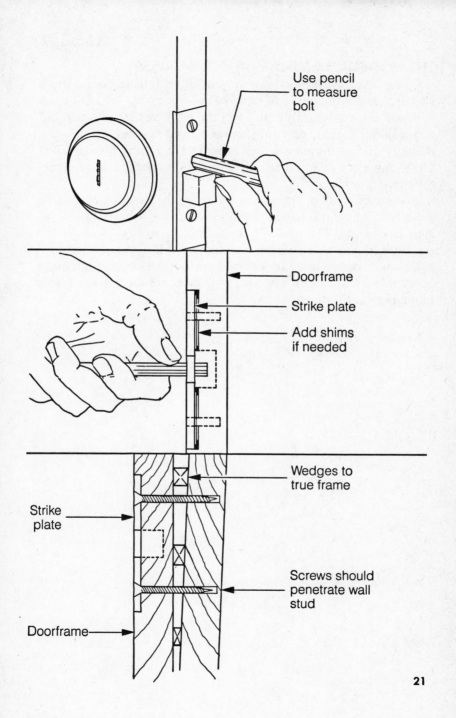

Use pencil to measure bolt

Doorframe

Strike plate

Add shims if needed

Wedges to true frame

Strike plate

Screws should penetrate wall stud

Doorframe

THE NOT-SO-DEAD BOLT (UNDER $10–$50)

Cheapie manufacturers often sell entry latches and thumb switches under the name of dead bolts. Not good.

These are recognizable to burglars, who can simply pop out any adjoining glass, reach inside, and twist the bolt open. Incidentally, increasing numbers of females are getting into the burglary business, and their slim wrists make such squirmy manipulation easier.

If there is glass in the door or nearby, get a genuine double dead bolt that can be opened only with a key, whether from inside or outside. Just remember, hide a spare key close to the doorway in case you ever need to let yourself out in a hurry.

The surface-mounted monsters shown opposite are sometimes good sale items under $10 and are often easiest for the home handyperson to install.

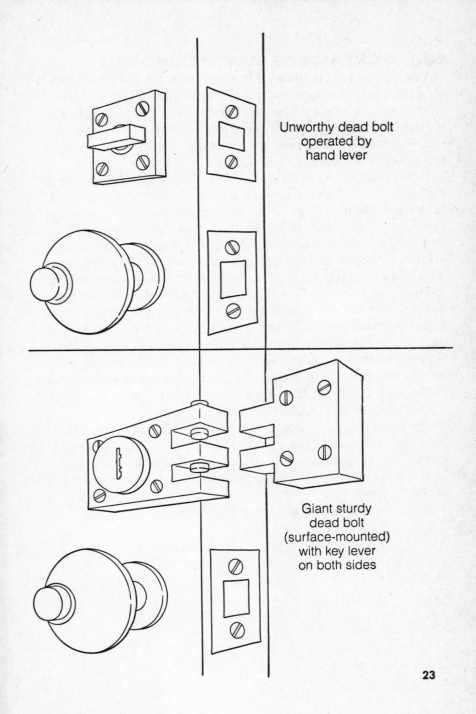

Unworthy dead bolt
operated by
hand lever

Giant sturdy
dead bolt
(surface-mounted)
with key lever
on both sides

BOLTS (HOMEMADE, $2; MANUFACTURED, $20)

You've probably seen tiny brass bolts and flip holders in blister-pack displays at supermarkets. They're known as barrel bolts. As holders for sewing baskets they're okay. For doors they're useless. The material used is invariably flimsy. The screws provided to hold them in position are about ½-inch long, made of soft brass or the mildest steel. Useless.

If you can tolerate bolts on the inner faces of your doors, then for heaven's sake use the biggest, ugliest monsters you can afford. If the bolt itself isn't as thick as a felt-tip-pen barrel and the screws aren't 1½ inches in length, don't waste your time installing them. Of course, as usual, if your door is a hollow-core model, you'll have problems locating firm areas for mounting any hardware. Tap near the edges of such doors to locate sturdy wood.

Think for a minute. One side of your door is now held in position by four hinges, each fastened by six to eight screws. That adds up to twenty-four or thirty-two husky screws. Now look at the opening side. What do you have? Two screws in a strike latch? Maybe two more in a dead bolt? What kind of nonsense is going on? Furthermore, most doorknobs and latches are fastened about halfway up the door. If you want to add bolts, why not fasten them at the top and bottom of the door?

The items illustrated opposite are reasonable facsimiles of bolts I made of mild steel for our first home, in Bucks County, Pennsylvania. The illustrations tell all. If painted black, the low-cost items resemble expensive wrought-iron fittings. If you don't tell anybody, I won't!

If you want to sound technical, they're called cane bolts.

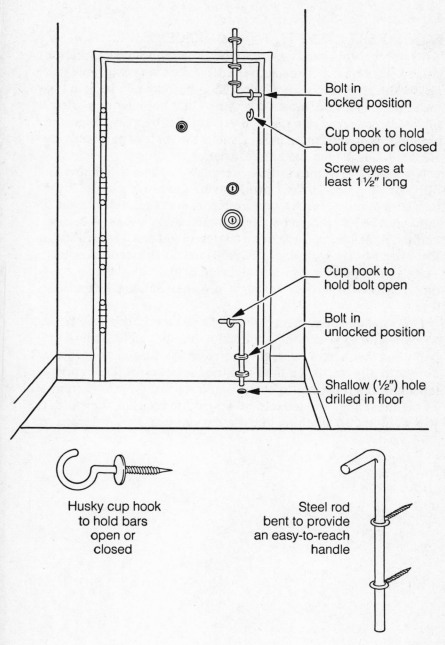

Bolt in
locked position

Cup hook to hold
bolt open or closed

Screw eyes at
least 1½" long

Cup hook to
hold bolt open

Bolt in
unlocked position

Shallow (½") hole
drilled in floor

Husky cup hook
to hold bars
open or
closed

Steel rod
bent to provide
an easy-to-reach
handle

NAILING THE DOOR STOP (FREE–50 CENTS)

The no-good blankety-blanks who broke into my son's house gained entry by prying back the vertical door stop near the latch on the side door and then manipulating the common latch out of the strike plate. Like most of the strips that hold doors in place, his had been tacked into position years earlier by a carpenter who used four flimsy finishing nails. Usually the coats of paint provide greater strength than the nail fasteners.

No matter. To correct this everyday weakness, hammer in thirty or fifty nails of your own, leaving the heads visible. If the burglar planning to attack your residence sees such a display he'll think maybe he's picked on a security nut and go someplace else.

If the door stop is made of metal you might consider drilling a few dozen holes with a good-quality metal drill and screwing many round-head screws into the frame, preferably long screws that will go all the way through into the studding behind the frame.

I know of one apartment dweller whose superintendent refused to allow him to pound in additional nails, saying, "It'll mark the paint." A few weeks later, the renter scratched and gouged the door stop himself, as if a thief had tried to break in. The superintendent hired a painter to come in and repaint the whole frame. In the meantime, the tenant had added the nails, as shown. But you wouldn't do anything like that, would you?

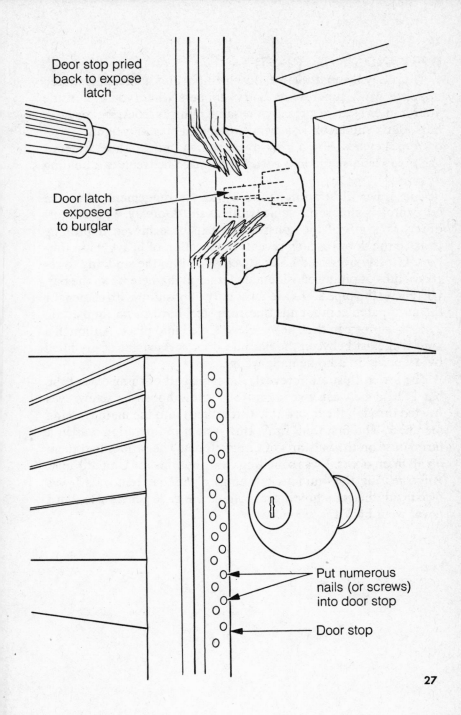

Door stop pried
back to expose
latch

Door latch
exposed
to burglar

Put numerous
nails (or screws)
into door stop

Door stop

PIPES AND RINGS ($2–$5)

They may be unattractive, but the pipes and holders illustrated opposite work superbly as entry stoppers when you are inside your home. They're virtually the same thing as frontier-type drop bars, but a smidgeon less primitive and lighter in weight.

Both sketches show a hacksawed ¾-inch (more or less) water or gas pipe just a shade longer than the space between two holding devices.

The upper illustration shows a tricky arrangement when the entry area is almost the same width as the doorway. The extraordinary strength of the construction can be achieved if probing close to the door framing reveals the location of heavy main timbers. Grossly oversized holes are chipped into the studding to receive stubs of piping considerably larger in diameter than the bar. Of course, the pipe stubs are set solidly in position with cement or the auto-patch compounds that turn steel hard in no time at all. The cross pipe can then be wiggle-waggled into place. Although a void will exist between the bar and door surface, it's easily filled by dropping in a homemade wedge.

The lower illustration reveals the same sort of thing except the bar is held between two monstrous screw hooks or screw eyes twisted through the doorframe (predrilled) into the main framing members. The first time I saw this system in operation was in a farmhouse on the outskirts of Philadelphia. The farmer had them on all main doors. I was soliciting contributions for United Fund. After hearing the ominous crashings of his bar removals I was faced with the gent, holding a shotgun. He gave generously, but I never went back for seconds.

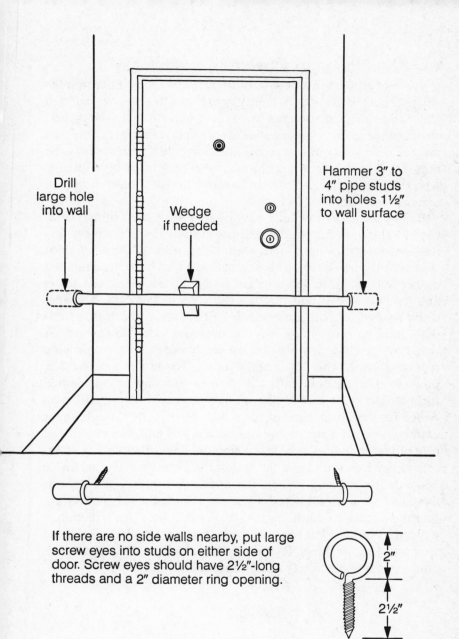

Drill large hole into wall

Wedge if needed

Hammer 3" to 4" pipe studs into holes 1½" to wall surface

If there are no side walls nearby, put large screw eyes into studs on either side of door. Screw eyes should have 2½"-long threads and a 2" diameter ring opening.

2"

2½"

29

THE VACATIONER'S SECURITY BARS (FREE–$5)

Summer cottages are regularly ripped off in the winter months when nobody is around. Not only does the cottage owner bemoan his losses, he faces double jeopardy when animals, large and small, move in through smashed doors and set up housekeeping and toilet facilities in mattresses and other things ignored by the burglars. At the right is an ultimate answer devised by a relative who shall be nameless because he wants his location to remain a secret even from you.

Before the first snow falls, my in-law moves everything portable of value into his windowless boathouse. It's built like a fortress and rests on piers over dry land. The inside of the entry door is pictured opposite. Note how three 2 × 4 bars have been pivoted on lag screws and joined together by "poly" rope knotted above and below holes drilled through the ends of the bars. The specially shaped brackets on one side of the inside doorframe studding face upward; those on the opposite side, downward. A common screen-door spring is fastened between hooks to provide tension to hold the bars canted upward when out of service, downward when duty calls. Observe how a tiny hole is drilled through the door directly below the topmost bar. A stiff wire poked through from the outside holds the bars up, though under extreme tension if the spring has been set to pull. On the hinged side of the door a tinier hole through the floor allows a fine stainless-steel wire to run from the end of the lowest bar into a crevice beneath the flooring. When the boathouse is full, the door is closed, the stiff wire is withdrawn, and *Wham,* the three bars slam into their brackets, until released by the pull wire. An inoperative key latch has been left in place to give passing burglars something to waste time picking. It works. The clever reader might even adapt this scheme to city use or apartments.

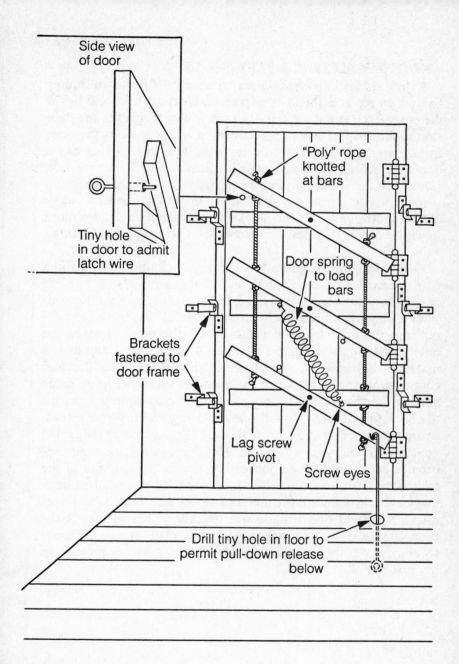

Side view of door

Tiny hole in door to admit latch wire

"Poly" rope knotted at bars

Door spring to load bars

Brackets fastened to door frame

Lag screw pivot

Screw eyes

Drill tiny hole in floor to permit pull-down release below

ANTIJIMMY PLATE (OR BAR) ($3–$5)

A slick gimmick to freak out any routine thief is this antijimmy bar, which replaces the door stop several inches above and below the entry latch and dead bolt. In case you've forgotten, the door stop is the strip of wood, sometimes metal, that stops the door from swinging all the way through the hole most of us call a doorway. Aficionados and trained purists, which we are not, would call the stuff doorjamb molding. Working carpenters and regular people simply say what it is—door stop, right? Usually it'll be lightweight wood about ⅜ inch thick and an inch or more in width, fastened in place by a couple of scrungy little finishing nails.

Even a fumbling felon can readily pry back the stop, slide in a plastic card, and "loid," or squeeze back, any everyday spring latch. He goes presto, your life goes changeo, like that. So consider slicing out a hunk of the stop by careful sawing and trenching into the door frame beneath it—neatly, now! Measure the hole you've dug out plus the thickness of the old strip and have a machine shop saw you a replacement in mild steel, drilled and countersunk to receive screw fasteners, as illustrated. I've made one, installed with nonremovable screws—you simply grind off the backside edges of slotted screws. Using Phillips-type screws, you install 'em first and then drill out the little ledges that enabled you to twist the screws in place. But there's an even easier approach. Measure up the door stop, guesstimate the depth of the trough, have the machine shop fabricate the bar, and then hack away at the wood until the metal plate fits. Any burglar who sees the shiny-bright one I made will quickly realize he hasn't the time, energy, or muscle to jimmy the door open. Besides, it looks so homemade, the occupant's probably not worth ripping off in the first place!

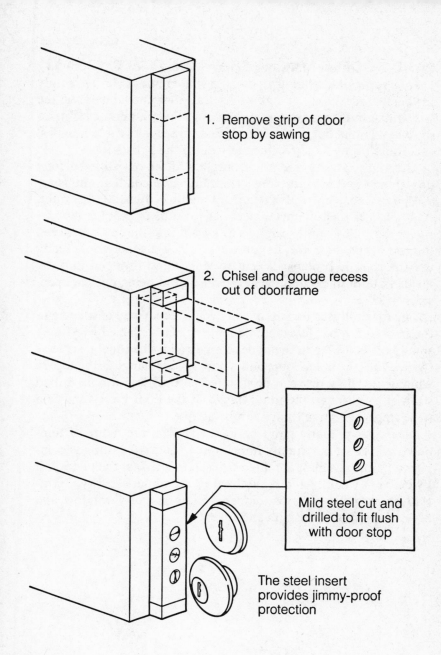

1. Remove strip of door stop by sawing

2. Chisel and gouge recess out of doorframe

Mild steel cut and drilled to fit flush with door stop

The steel insert provides jimmy-proof protection

PATIO DOORS—MAKING THEM IMMOVABLE (FREE–$1)

Any superwide sliding door is readily removable by simply lifting it and sliding it out of its tracks—removable until the owner fixes it in two minutes or less. And that's a minute less than most residential burglaries, which on average take three minutes, according to my expert witnesses west of the Mississippi.

There are cases on record of burglars lifting out wide balcony doors and lowering out pianos from high-rise condominiums!

You can beat 'em with a couple of methods, illustrated at right. At top is a ⅜-inch-diameter steel bar (or tube or pipe), a bit narrower than the door. It can be simply slid into the space between the top of the door and its top track. Zip. I assume you already use the routine broomstick, cut to length and dropped into the inside bottom track, to prevent the door from being pushed open, sideways.

The lower illustrations show an even cheaper way of locking in the patio door, but leaving it capable of being opened by you. A small hole is drilled in the upper frame and a sheet-metal screw is twisted into the hole. Some doors have a wide flange at the top, in which case the screw can be inserted vertically in a hole drilled straight up through the inner flange. If the door travels inside a wide track, the same things can be adapted.

Incidentally, many patio doors, or sliders, are made of tempered glass that is virtually impossible to cut. All cutting is completed before the glass is refired (thus, tempered) at the factory. If I were very wealthy and really freaked out about security, I'd install heavy plate glass or tempered glass in every window and door of my home, upstairs and down.

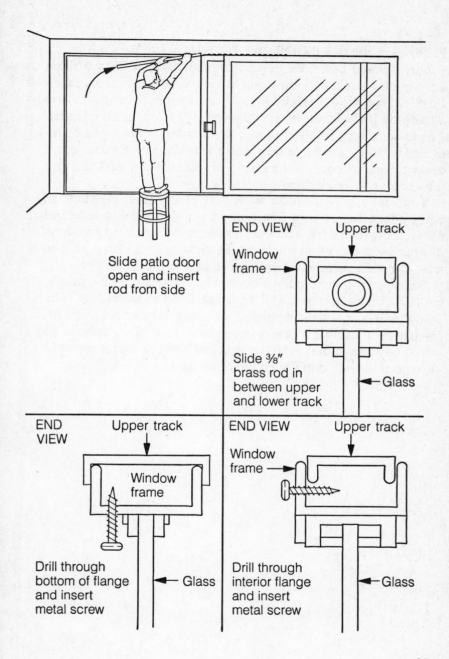

Slide patio door open and insert rod from side

END VIEW

Upper track

Window frame →

Slide ⅜" brass rod in between upper and lower track

← Glass

END VIEW

Upper track

Window frame

Drill through bottom of flange and insert metal screw

← Glass

END VIEW

Upper track

Window frame →

Drill through interior flange and insert metal screw

← Glass

PEEPHOLE IN THE DOOR (UP TO $4)

Surely you'd never, but never, open an exterior door without knowing for a certainty the exact identity of any caller. Although I like main entry doors with lights (windows) in them, it's always a trade-off if the windows are large enough to admit an intruder. The glass in very small windows, say 2 inches square, can be replaced with so-called one-way glass for below $10. Of course, it's one-way only if you, on the inside, are standing in darkness and the exterior is well lighted.

You really must provide some sort of eye-level peephole in entry doors. In my own first home I simply drilled a hole and plugged it with a cork. The next owner probably added an everyday hardware item that broadens the viewing area with a built-in lens. I've seen them advertised for as little as $1.

To be really functional, the device should look out on a mirror mounted on an opposite wall or porch, even a potted tree. The new wide-angle bull's-eye mirrors or commonplace rearview replacements available in every auto-parts store as cheaply as $3 would be ideal. And if ever you look out and the mirror seems to have been moved, don't open the door, no matter what!

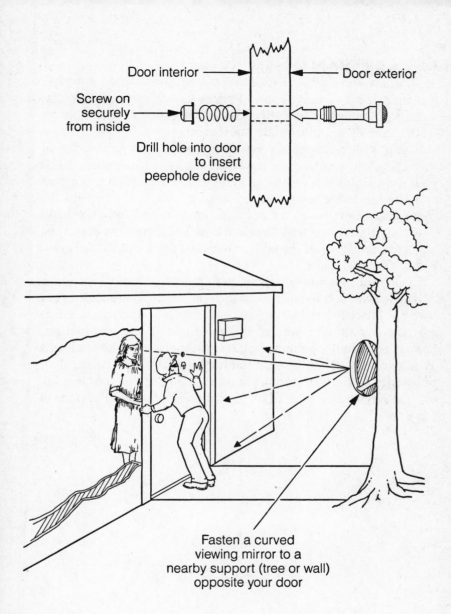

Door interior → ← Door exterior

Screw on securely from inside →

Drill hole into door to insert peephole device

Fasten a curved viewing mirror to a nearby support (tree or wall) opposite your door

37

THE DOOR CHAIN ($2–$5)

A variety-store door chain such as you see pictured opposite, top, isn't worth carrying home. They're usually packaged in blister cartons complete with tiny screws that wouldn't withstand an elbow push by a junior-grade housebreaker.

If you wish to impress your friends with your knowledge of such things, just show them how a chained door is opened. Twist your wrist through the opening and plunk a wad of chewing gum or putty inside the door, as far in as you can reach beyond the chain latch. Bury a rubber band in the gum and loop the band over the chain slider, well stretched out. Then close the door. The rubber band will pull the slider along the track until it falls out. Presto! You're inside.

Easier still, snip the taut chain with a good pair of wire cutters.

If, however, you like the idea of chain barriers, customize your own as illustrated below. Invest in a foot of superstrong hardened-steel chain with welded links as thick as you can tolerate. Search out a couple of monstrous screw hooks with shafts at least 1½ inches long. Now be sure the hook in the frame of the door penetrates all the way into the main studding. If the door is solid, run the screw hook in until its point dimples the outer surface of the door.

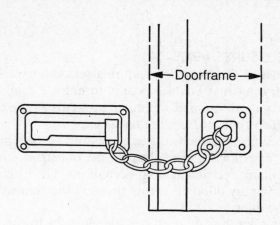

The Useless Door Chain

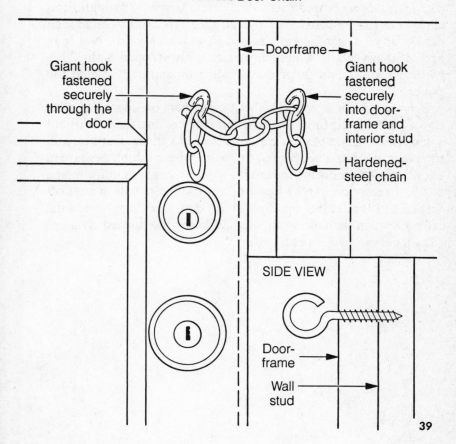

Giant hook fastened securely through the door

Giant hook fastened securely into door-frame and interior stud

Hardened-steel chain

Doorframe

SIDE VIEW

Doorframe

Wall stud

DOOR ENCLOSURES (FREE–$?)

Many homes in the snow belt feature a protruding or interior vestibule entryway that enables people to enter a kind of "air lock" to remove galoshes and wet outer garments without releasing too much costly heat from the residence.

If I still occupied a home with such a feature I'd be tempted to add permanent grillwork over glass on the outside door, which I'd fit out with an electric latching mechanism. Then I could see who was ringing my doorbell before pressing the "enter" button to unlatch the door.

In the sunny South and Southwest, the door enclosure is gaining in popularity. These are really little more than three-sided cages with tops, secured to the entry area. Genuine wrought-iron enclosures can be costly. Sharp-eyed shoppers can assemble such devices from discarded gates found in wrecking yards. Not long ago, near my place, a homeowner actually trapped a thief between his inner and outer doors, while he smilingly dialed the police.

Personally, I'm squeamish about using bars on doors and windows, or even visiting homes where they're installed. Without some readily operable release devices they can be deathtraps in the event of a fire. I've reached the point where I don't hesitate to ask any host to show me the family window-bar system if I'm at a party or reception. And I know of a homeowner who wasn't offended but thankful when I observed that in an emergency the release system he had installed could barely be opened by a gorilla, let alone by his petite wife.

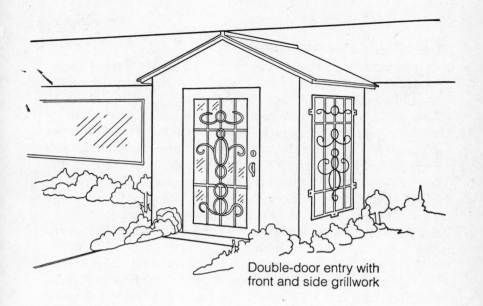

Double-door entry with
front and side grillwork

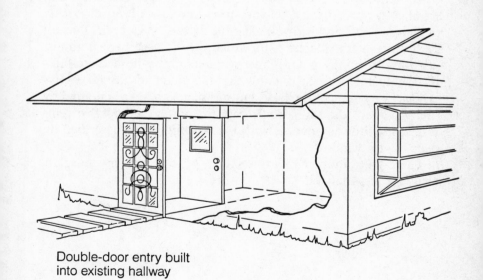

Double-door entry built
into existing hallway

41

THE TONE PAD (FREE–$40)

At present, the ultimate device for security systems, whether passive, active, or "just foolin' around," is the tone pad, usually resembling the three on the opposite page.

In auto-parts and electronics stores you can buy three-, four-, up to twelve-button models, some with lights and/or twist switches. In a working alarm system, of course, the buttons must be depressed in the correct sequence in order to activate or shut down the system. My friend the doctor has had a visible pad installed alongside each door. It does nothing but sit there and blink. The real tone pad, which causes one of his systems to do everything but shoot skyrockets if missed, is concealed behind the panel bearing his house number.

In my case, I have pads visible at front and rear doors and on the door panel of one car. All three are pure, unadulterated dummies that I cut with a hacksaw from an old tone pad given to me by a friend who is a telephone installer. I covered the letters and numbers with paint and set the strips into holes I cut alongside the house doors and below the handle on the '63 Corvair. I install such things with silicone glue, which can be used to seal almost anything to anything. Only the members of my immediate family, the doctor, and Harry know that my tone pads are fakes. Everyone else who sees the push buttons seems to be intimidated by them. I figure the same holds true for burglars. And I've reinforced my little toy guards with the flashing diode described on page 80, for windows.

There goes another of my secrets—how I scare my burglars away for less than $25.

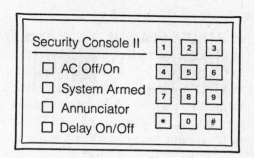

Security Console II

☐ AC Off/On
☐ System Armed
☐ Annunciator
☐ Delay On/Off

1	2	3
4	5	6
7	8	9
*	0	#

Expensive
touch pad
Console/Unit

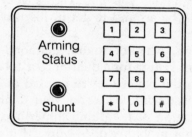

Arming
Status

Shunt

1	2	3
4	5	6
7	8	9
*	0	#

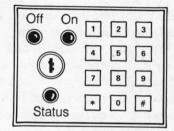

Off   On

Status

1	2	3
4	5	6
7	8	9
*	0	#

Telephone Touch Pad Device

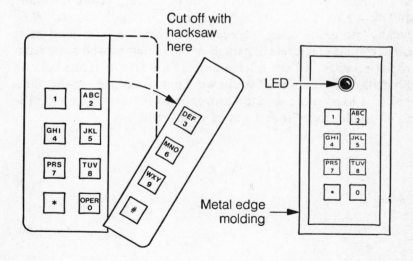

Cut off with
hacksaw
here

LED

Metal edge
molding

THE HARUM-SCARUM, NO-WORKUM DOOR LABEL

Mail-order ads, electronic shops, and even some well-known supply stores will sell you labels that read, "This Property Is Protected by the Grab 'Em/Catch 'Em Burglar Company."

Bunk. You know it's a phony label. The outfit that sold it knows it's just a scrap of paper. The burglar who spots it near your front door or car window has been reading the same ads and knows that you're really just kidding. He proceeds to break into your place because he's been watching you and knows your habits and knows when you won't be around to get in his way while he impoverishes you.

Most paste-on decals and labels, whether round, diamond-shaped, or preprinted in four colors, selling for a quarter to a dollar, are for a fact worth less than the paper they're printed on. Even an apprentice thief will whistle while he works your door open if he sees that you're counting on such a dumb subterfuge.

There is one label, however, that probably does work. If it's truly customized it may well deter thieves from going after your property. It's typed by you on sticky paper. *Please* don't simply copy the words that are given in the lower illustration opposite as an example. Make up your own. The police radio band is usually 140 through 176 megahertz. *N.C.* means "normally closed." *N.O.* means "normally open." *Frequency shifter* is a term used most often by manufacturers of garage-door openers as well as by security specialists. All the other numbers are simply make-believe. So make believe some of your own. Some folks *write* in the number of a local professional alarm-monitoring service in case the thief decides to try it as a test of your credibility.

PROTECTED
BY
ELECTRO
ALARM CO.

WARNING
"DAISY"
SECURITY
ALARM SYSTEMS

PROTECTED PREMISES

7045–1. Police– To order reset of
system call 140.67 megahertz, Band two.
System is N.C. with N.O. redundant
backup. Frequency shifter and S.A.
34587–0

In emergency call
555–1212

GARAGE DOORS ($1; ELECTRIC OPENERS, $100+)

When garage-door openers first came on the market, most of
the doors would open if a passerby happened to sneeze at the
correct frequency. No longer. For $150, plus or minus $50, you
can buy a sophisticated device that works the garage door automatically and provides unparalleled comfort, safety, and property
protection. After a telephone, the best buy in town. It turns on
lights ahead of the car operator and shuts them off automatically
a minute or more later, as you predetermine. The latest models
lock up your garage, and the superspecials will even sound a fire
alarm or carbon-monoxide alert if the car's engine does things it
should not do. They are a much better money investment than
the automobiles they protect, in my opinion.

Nevertheless, I promised you unusual security for small
money. The best I have seen recently is an electrical-outlet cover
plate, 6 inches in diameter, with an extra hole drilled in the center
for fastening it to the midpoint of a door using a round-headed
screw, with at least three small washers between the plate and the
door. Next, a small-diameter rod is bent at one tip so that it can
be slipped into one of the screw holes on the outside edge of the
plate. But first the rod has been cut to length and threaded
through some screw eyes that guide the unbent end into a hole
drilled into the top frame of the garage-door opening. A short
spring or a weight can be fastened to the opposite outside edge of
the plate to hold the rod in its most extended position. Now it's a
simple matter to drill, saw, or chip a slit through the door so that
a nail or screwdriver or pen can be inserted into that bottom hole
and then swung to shift the plate and cause the rod to be withdrawn. The hole in the door is covered by a working or fake hasp
and padlock, as shown.

Another option, sliding bolt locks, is shown below.

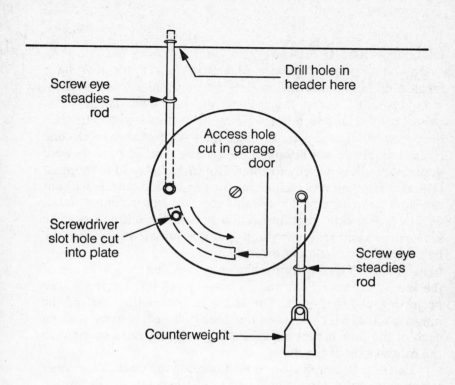

Drill hole in header here

Screw eye steadies rod

Access hole cut in garage door

Screwdriver slot hole cut into plate

Screw eye steadies rod

Counterweight

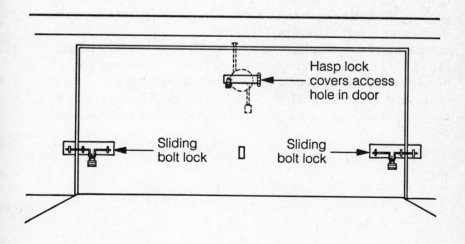

Hasp lock covers access hole in door

Sliding bolt lock

Sliding bolt lock

DOOR EXTRAS (FREE–$6)

On the opposite page are illustrated four items that have created endless conversation between me and certain visitors. You may enjoy incorporating them into your own system.

UPPER LEFT. There were a few—very few—times when our children were young—say, six through eight years of age—when one or more might be left briefly in the house alone. The orders were very clear. Allow nobody to enter. Got it? Nobody. Our youngest took that regulation to include me the day I stood outside without my door key, begging for admittance. My best response, later, was to drill a child-high inspection port in the entry door. The kids still remember the tiny iron grill that initiated them into the habit of self-protection at an early age.

UPPER RIGHT. The illustration shows a door hinge in which one of the screws is backed out and its head sawed off, leaving a stub projecting about ½ inch. The screw in the mating half of the hinge is removed. Now when the door is closed, a screw stub on each of the four hinges engages a hole, adding extra strength to the hinged side of the door.

LOWER LEFT. If there's a doorbell alongside the door, it's an easy job to extend the wires downward to another, larger bell button. In years gone by we trained our dog and cat to ring the bell by pushing the button with their noses. The cat often used her paw. Both animals learned within four weeks.

LOWER RIGHT. A standard, hand-held $5–$6 Freon horn alarm can easily be clamped in a homemade brace and fastened to the bottom panel of an exterior door. When the door is left ajar for ventilation it can be held by a brick or block. The blast will be terrifying if anyone tries to push the door open in a forceful manner.

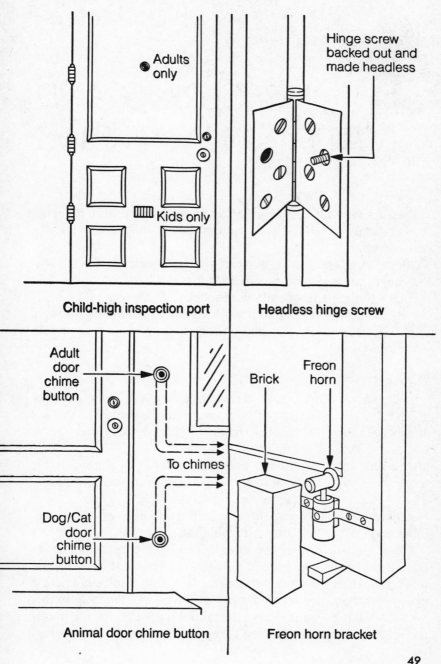

Child-high inspection port

Adults only

Kids only

Headless hinge screw

Hinge screw backed out and made headless

Animal door chime button

Adult door chime button

To chimes

Dog/Cat door chime button

Freon horn bracket

Brick

Freon horn

49

4

SECURING AND FORTIFYING WINDOWS

I've met very few police officers and security consultants who don't talk about windows as though they're telling you brand-new secrets.

"Some burglars cruise the streets at night looking into windows that might present good possibilities for break-ins tomorrow."

That's the most frequently mentioned old wheeze.

Nevertheless, if half of all household entries are made through unlocked or shabbily fastened windows, they must get our full attention. Okay?

THINK STUFF

Let's ponder other known facts about burglars. They prefer to go about their work without bumping into strangers, like the occupants of the home they're heisting. So there are daytime operators and nighttime specialists.

The daytimers have been known to roll up to a house with trucks or moving vans and empty a residence to the bare floors. The night prowlers seem to enjoy the extra thrill of getting into a residence where the occupants are sleeping, to lift everything portable and take off without disturbing the sleepers.

Donn Umber, one of my most dependable consultants, from the Crime Prevention Bureau hereabouts, surprised me with the news that when the officers snare one thief they can usually clear up, on average, twenty burglaries—at least that's the ratio in this area. The officers simply drive the criminal up and down a preselected grid of streets, and it isn't long before the burglar is saying,

"Hey, I got that brick duplex with the poinsettias without even disturbing their little dog. And over there, on the other side, same night, I got a wallet *that* fat with credit cards."

A review of past crime locations (usually called dot maps) will generally confirm the stories they hear from their arrestees. After a while, the researcher begins to realize that true professional criminals do take a certain pride in their work. Unless they are detected in action and provoked into some kind of counterattack, they won't engage in any rough stuff. Unfortunately, there's no certain way of knowing in advance whether *your* burglar is a tidy professional, a roughshod amateur, or, worst of all, a panicky crazy whose brain might be rotted out with drugs or some other sickness. They are the ones who don't even realize at times that their property assaults are escalating into heinous felonies like battery, rape, or homicide.

LETTING IN THE SUNSHINE

If I had done a fairly creditable job of securing my doors and windows only to discover some day or night that one or more strangers had somehow worked their way into my residence, I'd be ready for them if I heard them entering.

I'd do *nothing* to provoke them.

That would have been my carefully thought-through plan.

If the thief thought I was sleeping while he worked, I'd do nothing that might make him think otherwise. I regret that I have only one life to live, and to the greatest extent possible I plan to live it for at least a hundred more years.

If the thief knew that I knew what he was doing, I'd sit quietly until he had cleaned me out and had gone on his way. Then I'd work full tilt with the police to plop the crook behind bars while maybe I recaptured my possessions.

But long before those possibilities happened I'd have already taken some practical, routine, inexpensive steps to discourage the rascal(s) from crawling through my windows in the first place. Let's mention enough so that you might dream up some better ones, customized, all of your very own!

THE STICK IN THE WINDOW, REVISITED (FREE–$1)

The bottom section of a standard double-hung wooden sash can usually be raised for ventilation. The upper section all too often is firmly painted into place. If not, I'd be tempted to drill a hole through both side rails of the upper and lower sashes so they could be pinned together with ice picks or nails. With them moving as one, up and down, the opening could be adjusted small enough to deny any normal-size body room to squeeze through.

Again, the fastest, cheapest way of firming up the lower sash is to trim a broomstick or similar scrap of wood to fit snugly into the window channel.

Meanwhile, examine the thumb twist lock, if that's the style that's mounted on your windows. Usually, after years of wear, of condensation dripping down from the upper windowpanes, the lock halves are sitting in spongy wood. There's absolutely nothing wrong with moving the lock halves to the right or left of center if the wood is firmer there. Furthermore, I'd keep a heavy weight or hammer nearby so that the latches could be tapped firmly into closed position. The illustration suggests how such latches are often kicked off by the insertion of a thin blade and a few hammer taps. And let's assume throughout this section on windows that, whether renter or homeowner, you've at least packed the glass panes solidly into the frames with putty or other glazing compound, always with "points" pressed firmly into the wood before applying the goo. Points are the tiny metal widgets that hold windowpanes in place before the glazing compound is applied. And by the way, if you can't seem to get the compound smooth, keep dipping your putty knife in water as you work around the job. It's a cinch to do neatly.

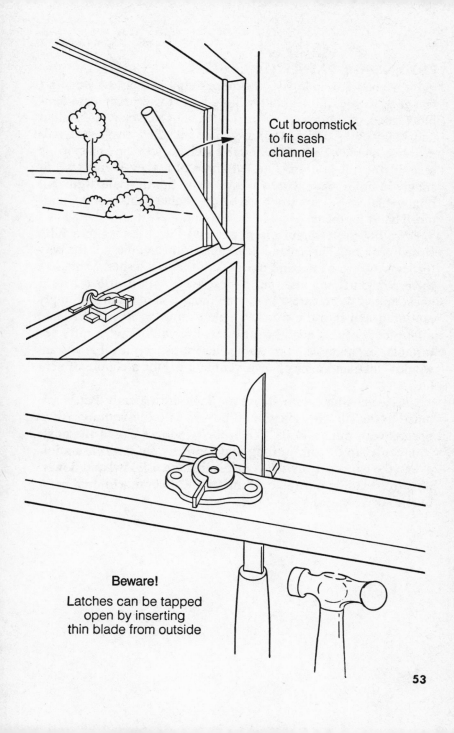

Cut broomstick
to fit sash
channel

Beware!

Latches can be tapped
open by inserting
thin blade from outside

PEGGING THE SASHES (50 CENTS–$4)

If the notion of nailing your windows shut permanently doesn't feel good to you, think about drilling holes to accommodate double-headed, or, more correctly, duplex, nails that can be installed and removed as desired, handily. The nails, by any name, will measure roughly 2½ inches, about 2 inches up to the first stop, as seen in the illustration. I tested three and they seemed to fit snugly in holes made with a ³⁄₁₆-inch drill, but the nails were still removable. So if yours wobble a bit, bend them a hair in the middle. That'll fix them.

First, however, wham the upper and lower sashes into fully closed position. Then plan ahead and drill the holes all the way through the cross rails and uprights of the two sashes. Some like them straight, I suppose, but almost every time I drill a hole it goes slanted. Who cares? I've done them without a drill. Simply tap-tap a nail into the wood, wiggle it out, tap it in again, and after plenty of this good healthy exercise you'll have a nifty adjustable, expandable, retractable, insertable, removable instant window lock and controller of ventilation—for a couple of pennies.

The lower illustration shows an angle-iron gizmo that is fastened to the sill with screws and pegged into the bottom sash as needed with duplex nails. When the window's closed the angle iron can keep it from rattling and be fitted out with insulation. When the window's up it aids in keeping the fishbowl and flowerpots from sailing out the opening when the grandchildren come over to drive you silly.

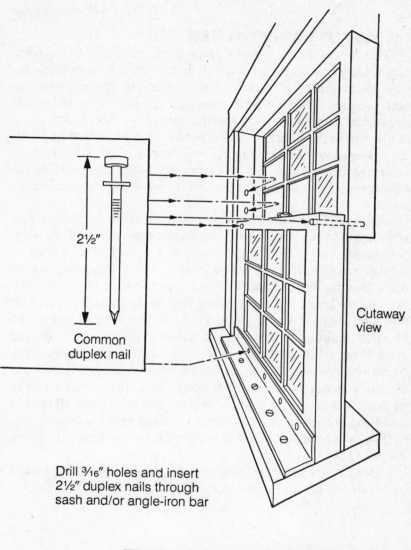

2½"

Common
duplex nail

Cutaway
view

Drill ³⁄₁₆" holes and insert
2½" duplex nails through
sash and/or angle-iron bar

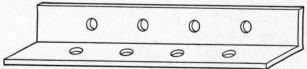

THE MOVABLE WINDOWS (FREE–$?)

When I was working my way through school as a musician, playing several nights each week in dance bands, I never knew for sure what kind of potential firetrap we might find ourselves in each evening. It became an automatic reaction to scout the premises casually and make very specific plans for escape in the event of any fire or panic or other emergency. That habit remains with me to this day. Whether it's a movie house, concert hall, or a new residence I'm visiting, I have a darned good idea of several logical escape routes in case they're needed by me or my companions in a hurry.

Whenever I buy or rent a house or apartment, one of my first activities is to make sure every window opens wide, all the way, without sticking. I don't care if I chip the paint, since I plan to repaint anyway. Do you know how to make windows easy to open? See the illustration. (1) Tap a chisel or wide blade between the window frame and the molding that holds the sash in place on one side. Remove the molding. (2) Slide the window out of the opposite molding and swing the window inward. Now do the same thing with the upper sash, by removing the beading between the two sash channels. You may have to pry it out, but usually it is not nailed in. Now you're ready to work on all the surfaces that have been binding. Scrape and sand away all the old paint and lubricate the wood for easy sliding with a tallow candle.

If the windows are metal casements, treat the hinges to a few drops of oil.

Now that you have the windows easy to open, you can proceed to install any of the locking devices that hold them shut.

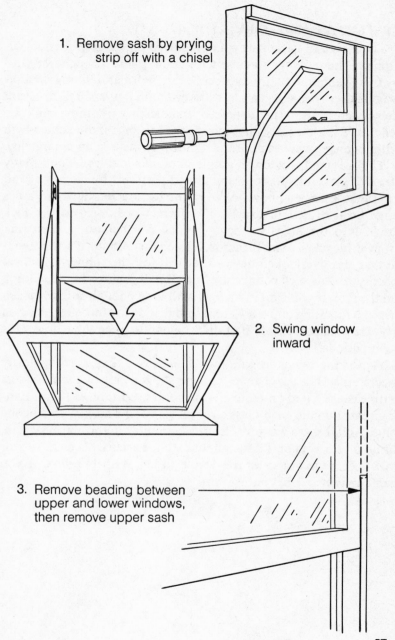

1. Remove sash by prying strip off with a chisel

2. Swing window inward

3. Remove beading between upper and lower windows, then remove upper sash

CASEMENTS AND LOUVERS (FREE–$5)

The standard casement window hangs on hinges, like a door. Some of them open and close with crank handles, anchored shut by twist latches. Usually the handles are worn and falling off anyway. If they're not, use a screwdriver or allen wrench to unfasten the setscrew. Put the detached handles where they can't be reached from outside, but store the crank or handle somewhere within convenient reach of the window for use in an emergency.

The louvered window, a tangle of cranks and levers and many strips of glass, tilts to open and closed positions by the same kind of crank described above. Note in the illustration how two holes have been drilled in exactly the correct positions on the lock latch. Into the holes we have popped a superstrong open link from a bicycle or small motorcycle chain. Again, it's the unexpected and overlooked device that will foil the robber. My local bike store sells such connecting links for 50 cents to $1, depending on the size. If you can find a link with long enough stubs you can slip the retaining clip over the inserted ends for those times when you are going on vacation or don't intend to open the window for long periods.

As for the louvered windows themselves, they are hopelessly vulnerable. The glass strips can be slipped out of their holders with ease. If I had any louvered windows, I'd replace them. Failing that, I'd glue each glass strip into its end braces with silicone glue. And if there was any electrical circuitry in the alarm system, or no alarm system, I'd install an exterior security screen, real or fake (see page 66), over the whole thing. With burglars, if you can't convince 'em, confuse 'em.

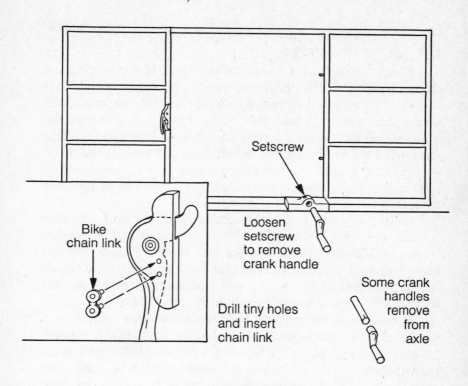

Setscrew

Loosen
setscrew
to remove
crank handle

Bike
chain link

Drill tiny holes
and insert
chain link

Some crank
handles
remove
from
axle

Louvered Windows

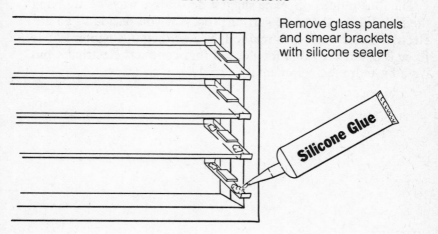

Remove glass panels
and smear brackets
with silicone sealer

Silicone Glue

THE FOIL STRIP ($5–$10)

A plastic or aluminum-foil strip might well be the single most alarming gadget to fall under the eyes of a would-be robber. If it looks fresh and well maintained, it's very unlikely the crook will take a chance on jimmying the door or fooling around with the window that displays the outline of a strip of foil. The type that has proved most effective through decades of service is the metal strip that loops each window and connects into a genuine alarm system. But it can be expensive, as you'll observe in the next chapter.

I have had great luck using ordinary plastic foil, chrome-colored, available in ³⁄₁₆-inch width at almost any photographic store. A 1200-foot roll retails for less than $12 and provides enough to foil two, three, or even four small homes. (If you decide to share the cost with someone, you must warn them to keep our secret.) This trick is so effective that the landlord of a home we rented nearly tore up my lease. He'd neglected some maintenance work and finally got around to the job when we were out of town. He had a passkey, but when he saw the metallic-looking strips on the windows and doors, he was too panic-stricken to attempt an entry. I'd ruined his day, not his property as he soon discovered.

The illustrations opposite suggest decorative ways of applying the foil. It'll be the same sort of process if you decide to go all-electric or electronic with real foil, as described in Chapter 5. The price is about the same for the foil that conducts electricity, but it's a bit more temperamental to apply.

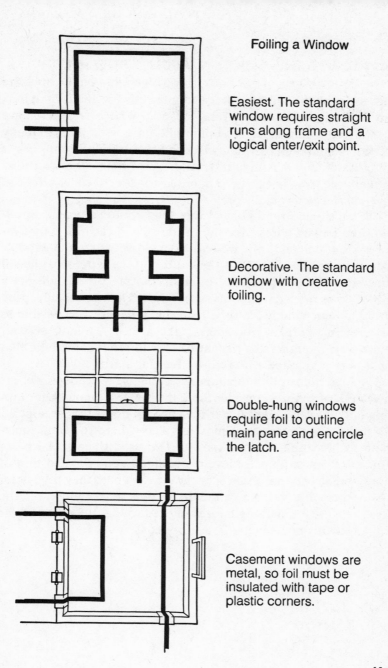

Foiling a Window

Easiest. The standard window requires straight runs along frame and a logical enter/exit point.

Decorative. The standard window with creative foiling.

Double-hung windows require foil to outline main pane and encircle the latch.

Casement windows are metal, so foil must be insulated with tape or plastic corners.

WIRE LOOPS AND WOODEN WEDGES (FREE–$1)

Of all the gadgets in this book, those illustrated on the opposite page are probably the cheapest and most unexpected for the burglar who might be casing your location. The wire strands are nothing more than the lightest of brightly insulated wires that any passing telephone repairman will hand you from his scrap bag if you ask politely. A couple of feet of four- or six-conductor telephone hookup wire can be purchased for 5 or 6 cents a foot at your nearby electronics store.

Wind a single strand about 1 foot long around a pencil. Install two such looped wires over the inside sill on each of your windows. Hold one end in place with sticky tape where the window drops into the space behind the sill. Loop the wire over the sill and fasten the other end out of sight underneath the sill. Set a pair of wires in place about 2 inches apart. Then go outside, peek through your window, and be sure the wires are very visible to any peeping burglar who might take a close-up look at your house with intent to steal. What he should see is something that looks very much like a hooked-up burglar alarm.

The lower illustration demonstrates the use of wooden wedges sawed out of scrap. I consider them the greatest gimmick for tapping into window slides, under the edges of doors that are open a few inches for ventilation, almost anyplace where you want something to hold tighter if it's moved. I've used them to keep car windows from rattling, for leveling tabletops, and for a vast list of other nonsecurity purposes. Depending on where they'll be used, I paint them either to match the things they're wedging or, in the case of security, a flaming fluorescent red so that the next burglar will know this homeowner is security-conscious.

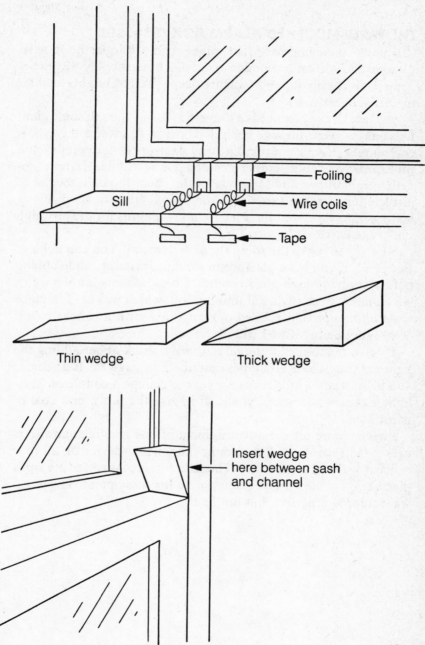

Foiling

Sill

Wire coils

Tape

Thin wedge

Thick wedge

Insert wedge here between sash and channel

THE WALL-MOUNTED ALARM BOX ($1–$10)

Another passive device that might send a burglar hopping is nothing more than a wooden or metal box, roughly 12 inches wide, 18 inches high, and 6 inches deep, painted bright, screaming, fire-engine red.

The face of the box needs a louvered look as though some giant noisemaker were lurking behind it, ready to arouse the whole community. If you can't find a rusty fixer-upper for pennies in a junkyard, you can assemble a reasonable facsimile. Hammer together a small box and sand it smooth. Then slap on a section of old shutter or some venetian-blind strips, fitted to slant downward as if to ward off rain. Prepare hook mounts for the box high under the eaves.

Now try to make the thing shine, like metal. You can achieve this result if you have patience in sanding, priming, and rubbing before applying high-gloss enamel. I once saw such a device in silver, made by applying aluminum foil, which was held in place with white glue and rubbed out smoothly with a rubber roller. Very intimidating. But *I* still prefer red.

To give the thing additional authority, think about adding the light-emitting diode (IC type) described on page 80. It'll require you to crawl up a ladder once a year to change a couple of flashlight batteries and, while you're at it, give the box a new coat of paint.

I have before me the advertisement of one genuine alarm-box maker ($30 stripped) that recommends such a device on all four exterior walls of a residence. The four I made—two for my son's place, two for mine—cost a total of $3 for spray paint. The wood was scrap. Not perfect, but not bad!

The Alarm Box

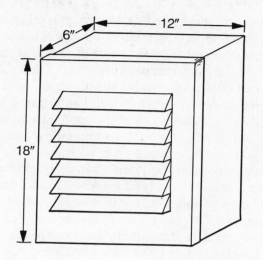

Wooden or
metal box
painted
flame red

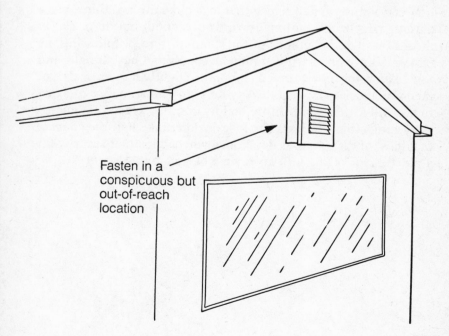

Fasten in a
conspicuous but
out-of-reach
location

SECURITY SCREENS, FACT AND FICTION (FREE–$60)

The security screens mentioned in the chapter on louvered windows are nothing more than insect-type window screens through which a fine electrical wire has been threaded, up and down, in and out, in the same manner as any of the other strands in the screen. Usually the starting and finishing ends of the alarm wire are terminated in a reed switch, which is illustrated "in the raw" on page 83. It's tiny enough to be dropped into the groove around the perimeter of the screen, the same groove that holds the plastic strand that retains the screen in its frame.

These are always custom-made items. A good-quality alarm-ready security screen approximately 24 inches wide and 48 inches tall might cost upward of $60, plus installation, if needed.

When the screen is set in place, a small magnet is fitted in the wood of the window to hold the switch closed or open, as you'll read in Chapter 5. If the screen is cut with a knife or lifted out of position, the alarm will sound.

If you simply want a screen that *looks* like the real thing, use a darning needle and pull many yards of smooth button or carpet thread through the strands of the standard screen, following the pattern shown in the illustration. Keep your lines straight and true. The color of the thread should be slightly lighter or darker than the screen to be visible. Any burglar with an ounce of experience will hit the road before he hits into the screen that guards your vulnerable window. The rascals don't take half the chances that most of their victims do. Homeowners take their security for granted. Crooks take full advantage of such opportunity.

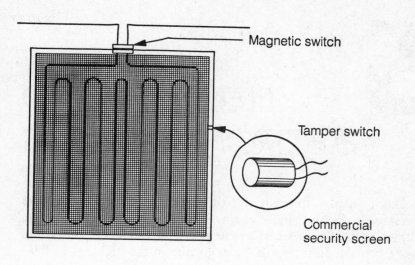

Magnetic switch

Tamper switch

Commercial
security screen

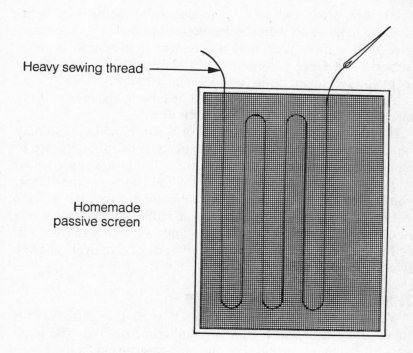

Heavy sewing thread

Homemade
passive screen

5

ELECTRICAL AND ELECTRONIC SYSTEMS

Has it occurred to you that in this era of high technology I have been recommending nails, chains, bars, and broomsticks as basic components of your security systems? Well, the fact is, they often work better than things that can go ring in the night, as in false alarms.

Oh sure, along the way we made casual mention of light-emitting diodes and switches that seemed to be begging for electrical energization. Well, here we are. The razzle-dazzle is about to begin, but I beg you not to let it alarm you, no matter how inept you feel about do-it-yourself voltage gadgets.

You can hook up the gizmos we'll be talking about even if the mention of electricity makes you a bit dizzy.

If you're strictly out of electrical or electronic things you may be somewhat disoriented for the next couple of pages. But try to hang in there. Get a feel for how these things are supposed to work. There's no pain involved. If you're like my pal the doctor, you'll wind up buying factory merchandise anyway, but at least you'll know what you're buying. If you're like my electronics-bug neighbor Harry, you'll be itching to improve on my suggestions.

The fact is, you've probably got a bunch of electrical gadgetry lying around your place already.

THINK ABOUT THE POSSIBILITIES

You have lamps in your home. If used thoughtfully with timers, they represent high-qualty anticrime devices. The same goes for radios, record players, and tape-cassette machines. I once wired a machine shop using clothespins as electrical switches.

68

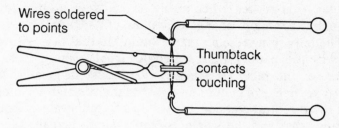

Wires soldered to points

Thumbtack contacts touching

As long as the windows of the shop were not tampered with, my chain of clothespins stayed closed, the electrical circuit was intact and the horns didn't blow.

The fire alarm was a slight variation on the theme. A different set of clothespins was held in the open position, their contacts separated by lumps of beeswax. Heat or flame would melt the wax, which would allow the contacts to touch and set the electrical circuit going to sound the siren.

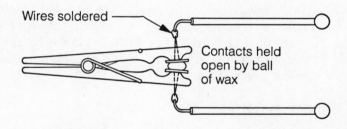

Wires soldered

Contacts held open by ball of wax

Believe it or not, you've just read about the whole process in any alarm system. There are four component parts in any system. They each respond to changing conditions.

1. The clothespins are the switches, sometimes open, sometimes kept closed. When something happens to change that normal condition, things happen to ring alarms or other forms of alert. We won't call them clothespins anymore. They're known nowadays as sensors or detectors.

2. For the first primitive system I built, the boss or his assistant turned it on or off from outside the building by poking a pencil through a hole in the wall, thus prodding a switch on or off.

Nowadays that master switch would be called the arming device, nothing but a thing to change condition, off/on/off.

3. The only thing resembling a "brain" in that original relic I built was the battery that sensed a signal coming from the switches or the relay (which we will discuss in greater detail shortly). A change of condition, right? In today's high-technology world those central components would be complicated elements in a fancy case and the whole assembly would be called a controller.

4. The bells, horns, and sirens have become sophisticated with the passage of time, too. Now there are all kinds of options available, including automatic dialing machines to alert a central monitoring station or the police. This part of the alarm system is called the annunciator.

These are the four parts of every alarm system. The final mention of my own ancient system must be the admission that I had no idea when I contrived it that it had an offbeat element of high tech. If anybody attempted illegal entry into that old machine shop, the clothespins would not only be opened, they'd be destroyed. Any criminal could not shut down the horns by simply closing the door or window in a hurry. You'll realize the value of that arrangement in a minute.

FOR THE DO-IT-YOURSELFER

Here is a diagram of a very routine open-circuit alarm:

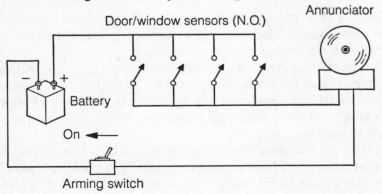

Door/window sensors (N.O.)

Annunciator

Battery

On

Arming switch

Turn the arming device (switch) to "on" and you'll hear the annunciator (bell) if any of the sensors (switches) are closed at any of the doors or windows. That's fine for a test, but it's not so good if an intruder can shut off your alarm by simply closing the door or window just entered illegally. We'll add an element called a relay and thus have a controller (brain) for our alarm system. The next diagram illustrates it. When electrical current flows through the wire coil in the relay, its core is magnetized and snaps the switch contacts to a second position.

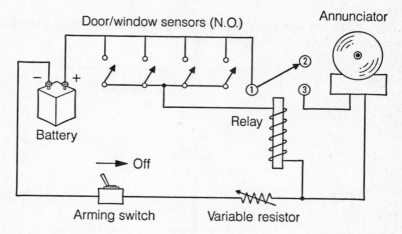

Relays have a beguiling characteristic. It takes a healthy punch of voltage to make one wake up and snap a contact lever to a new position. But once the contact has landed, it requires very little current to hold it there. Often it's easier to interrupt the power supply and let the built-in spring pull the contact back to rest than it would be to add on another set of windings to jerk it home by magnetic action.

In the sketches you can easily determine the values of the resistances if you have your component parts evaluated and then apply Ohm's law. Remember it?

Resistance (in ohms) is equal to the voltage (in volts) divided by the current (in amperes), or $R = E/I$.

If in doubt, ask your nearest high-school student.

In the diagram of the system with the relay, the arming device is in the "on" position. If a normally open sensor is closed by the action of a moving door or window, it sends current instantly through the relay (which is now the controller), which snaps the contacts from 1-2 (open) to 1-3 (closed). Wham! The annunciator is in the circuit, which simply means the bell starts ringing and will remain ringing until the battery runs down, a timer stops it, or someone comes running to shut down the system and reset it. Got the idea?

Let's examine the same sort of thing using a normally closed system, seen here in primitive form:

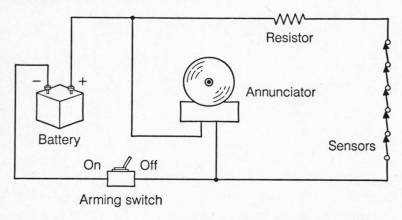

The arming device is seen here in the open (off) position. Mentally close it. You'll observe that the sensors, normally closed switches, are in fact creating a short circuit of sorts, which uses up the battery's power as heat in the limiting resistor. But look what happens when a sensor is opened. The short circuit is gone and the power is able to rush through to the annunciator, in this case a bell, which rings. It could be a siren that howls or a loudspeaker that goes "yelp, yelp, yelp."

The professional burglar and handy amateur can usually sense a normally closed (N.C.) or normally open (N.O.) system. So let's confuse him and use both systems in one circuit, and maybe add a fire-alarm (heat-sensitive) sensor at the same time, as shown in the next diagram:

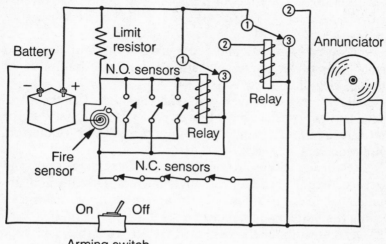

Arming switch

This system has an extra capability. When break-in artists set out to steal from a residence, they carry magnets and compasses in their pockets. The compass will swing wildly in the presence of a magnetic switch, and the magnet can be used quickly to bridge a gap if a switch is opened accidentally. Now, with a mixture of normally open and normally closed, the burglar will wind up a very frustrated fellow indeed. Also, a new style of sensor, called bias, will sound an alarm if any alien magnet is brought near it.

Let's assume you decide to wire your residence with some adaptation of the two-relay burglar alarm just illustrated, our most sophisticated offering thus far.

The prices are a range of discount to high retail as estimated by the security whizzes of General Supply Electronics in Los Angeles, California, mid-1983.

6-volt lantern battery	$1–$3
6-volt relay	$2–$4
6-volt alarm bell	$5–$15
6 assorted magnetic window sensors	$1–$4 (each)

Door switches and fire sensor	$2–$7 (each)
Master switch (arming device)	$1–$3
2-conductor wire @ 5 cents a foot	
Limiting resistor (15,000 ohms)	25 cents maximum

If you were to wire up a half dozen windows and two doors and used 150 feet of wire, you could still do the whole job for about $30–$60, including insulated staples.

General Supply Electronics will send you a list of all the materials you might consider including in your system if you describe your wishes to its Homemakers' Division, 2202 Pico Boulevard, Santa Monica, CA 90405.

Jeff Hellman, licensed consultant to General Supply and dozens of major corporations, governmental agencies and uncounted hundreds of householders, agrees with the concept of keeping the burglars off balance.

"They know about the systems that are available," he says. "But they can never be sure exactly what components have been put together. They don't know for certain whether a bell will ring indoors or outdoors or both. Maybe it'll be a siren. Maybe it'll be a silent alarm that dials automatically to a monitoring station. In some cities it is still okay to install automatic dialers that telephone direct to the police." Ask for a ruling from your local police if in doubt about legalities.

Hellman examined the systems in my residence as well as those at the doctor's and Harry's places. He was admittedly awed by the doctor's lavish installation of three very professional and differing systems. He showed the doctor how to readily interchange all the alarms with all of the detectors and annunciators.

"Your doctor friend's biggest problem will be trying to remember which combination is the active one this week," he commented laughingly. As for Harry's house, jammed with homemade electronic trips, traps, and surprises, "It's simply the ultimate in overkill," Hellman observed. "Actually, however, there's not too much in Harry's residence that can't be done by a new gadget that came on the market recently, American-made, miniature, and not much larger than a pack of cigarettes."

The control module, costing $35, and basic accessories can be obtained by writing directly to Jeff Hellman, P.O. Box 6421, Beverly Hills, CA 90212.

FROM ELECTRIC TO ELECTRONICS

With the arrival of transistors, devices such as Hellman's tiny controller became possible. If all of the relays in the earlier diagrams leave you somewhat bewildered, let's look at a single semiconductor that will perform all the relay functions. The one pictured here is made from specially treated sand that has been purified, then adulterated with just the right amount of foreign substance to give it unusual properties in conducting electricity. It will act as a switch, conductor, controller, and voltage regulator, all in one tiny package. We refer to it descriptively as a gate rectifier.

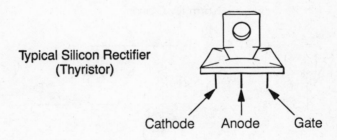

Typical Silicon Rectifier
(Thyristor)

Cathode   Anode   Gate

When the rectifier is nonconducting it's just like an open switch. When we push its gate, electrically, it closes to conduct electricity, so now it's a closed-circuit switch.

The most interesting characteristic of thyristors (silicon-controlled relays, or SCRs) is that once the gate has been opened, it stays that way even if the gate voltage is cut off. The system must be shut down and set for action from the beginning. It's a tough system to beat. We can make a burglar alarm out of it, as seen in this diagram:

Electronic Alarm

Normally Open

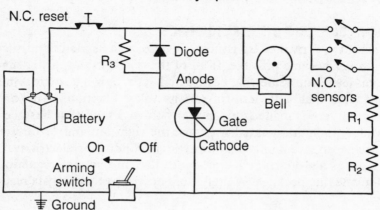

Normally Closed

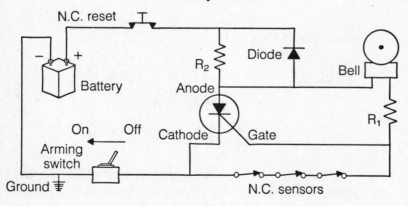

All the sensors in the open system will operate the gate if any one of them is closed. Instantly, a positive voltage reaches through resistance 1, whaps the gate and the thyristor "fires," sending current via anode and cathode to the bell, which keeps ringing because of the diode and resistor in its circuit. It will keep ringing until the battery runs down or an optional timer shuts it off, or the system is disarmed and reset with the little momentary-disconnect push button.

A similar system, though normally closed, is seen in the same diagram. Now the gate terminal remains connected to the cathode or ground as long as the sensors stay closed. But open one and the gate is disconnected from ground, a positive voltage zaps through resistance 1, closing the gate, causing the thyristor to fire, thus sounding the bell. The size of resistance 1 limits the gate current, the diode protects against big voltage peaks, and resistance 2 keeps the anode current flowing once the system has been activated. Again, it'll have to be shut down (disarmed) and reset after all the switches (sensors) have been closed once again.

Increasingly, community ordinances are requiring that alarm systems turn themselves off automatically after, say, ten or fifteen minutes of noisemaking. In these diagrams, timers would be wired into the reset switches, or arming circuits, allowing for automatic or manual control. In small systems timers might add an additional $10–$15 to the original investment, well worth it. Many cities are fining false-alarm offenders. Exotic versions of timers will restart the system noisemaking if human assistance is not aroused. Believe it or not, burglars have been known to deliberately trip alarms, wait for the batteries to run down or shut down, and then proceed to their work. Let's get back to our own, okay?

You've now had the basic course in electronic burglar-alarm systems.

Consultant Hellman reminds us of the variety of other modes that are available, but probably beyond the capabilities of most do-it-yourselfers. Infrared or heat detectors will sense body heat at distances up to 150 feet, and they'll sound alarms if the body shouldn't be there. They're usually called P.I.s or passive infrareds.

Microwave detectors emit signals and expect them to bounce back without interruption; otherwise, they fire off an alarm. You may not know it, but when you enter a supermarket door it opens because you've interrupted its microwave beam and it's told the receiving device not to ring a bell but rather to start a motor that'll open the door for you. You're being microwaved constantly, like it or not.

Another type of space protector, called active ultrasonic, emits sound waves above the range of the human ear. If the sounds don't make their "loop of security" undisturbed, they'll trigger alarm systems.

As you're about to see on the following pages, there are many styles of arming devices, sensors, power supplies, annunciators, alarm schemes, and status reporters, wireless and otherwise. Immediately ahead lie the interesting things you might wish to adapt to your own residential or office use for zero cost or very small budgets, according to the tools you have available and your handiness with them, your interest, and your curiosity about what makes things work.

SCARE-AWAY NEON BULB ($1–$4 FOR AC MODELS)

My neighbor Kay insists that the neon-bulb set I made for her windows saved her from a major break-in, because her house is the only one of a cluster of three that wasn't plundered in a terrible rash of burglaries last summer. The tiny bulbs pictured in the illustration sell for 25 to 50 cents each. They'll operate on a minuscule amount of current in the neighborhood of 90 volts. Hence, a homeowner who buys them from General Supply or any local electronics store must wire a small resistor of about 200,000 ohms (200K) into the line before plugging the assembly into a standard light socket. No, they don't blink, but they can be seen glowing even in daylight, as though something mighty alarming is hooked into them, just waiting. Kay asked me to make her six more for her friends. Instead, I made her a sketch, not half as good as the one on the opposite page, and she bought the materials and soldered them up, taped them, and glued them with red plastic covers in one afternoon. Kay is well into her seventies and had never held a soldering iron in her hand before.

Hookup for Neon Bulb

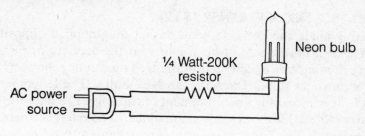

Neon bulb

¼ Watt-200K
resistor

AC power
source

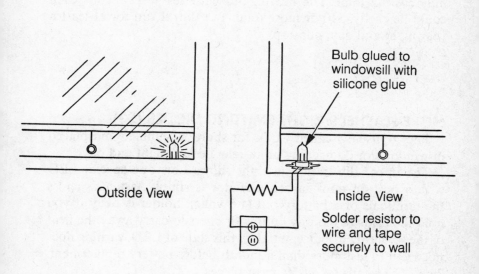

Outside View

Bulb glued to
windowsill with
silicone glue

Inside View

Solder resistor to
wire and tape
securely to wall

PORTABLE NEON FLASHER ($12)

Harry made the portable neon flasher diagrammed opposite. He leaves it on the seat of his car or near the accelerator pedal, where the shadows heighten its blinking. You can buy the parts at any electronics store. Insist on the NE2 bulbs. The letters *mfd.* stand for microfarad, a measurement of capacity. The letters *meg* mean million. (Megohm = a million ohms.) The reference here is to resistance. The bulbs, capacitors (or condensers), and resistors may cost $2 total. The hearing-aid batteries at 22½ volts each could be costly, $10 or more total. But they'll run for at least a year night and day, nonstop.

MORE FLASHERS: LIGHT-EMITTING DIODES ($3)

They're usually called LEDs for short. Assembled and placed in windows or doors, they blink relentlessly, night and day.

The upper illustration at right shows how one special LED with a built-in mini-flasher-oscillator is simply fastened across the terminals of a battery cell (1.5 volts). Solder is okay if you hold the leads of the tiny bulb with pliers to carry away the heat of the soldering iron. Regrettably, this style of LED warning does not seem to last more than a month before battery replacement. The LED retails for $1.50, most places.

A better style is shown in the lower illustration. The soldering is done into the socket for an eight-pin integrated circuit (IC). An LM 3909 IC, shown here, sells for less than $1.20. If you've never wired an IC before, this would be an easy one to start out on. The condenser (capacitor) is 47 mfd. Low, low voltage rating, even 3 watt/volts will do. The switch is optional, because with this circuit the bulb will blink for a year or more if connected to one simple D cell of reasonable quality.

The parts are available through General Supply Electronics, which advertises LEDs in yellow, green, and white as well as the usual red.

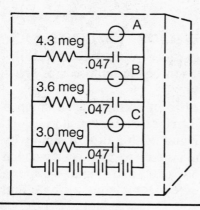

Portable Neon Flasher

Requirements:

3 tiny neon bulbs, type NE2
3 condensers, .047 mfd.
3 resistors, 4.3 meg
         3.6 meg
         3.0 meg
4 hearing-aid batteries
   of 22½ volts each,
   with holders

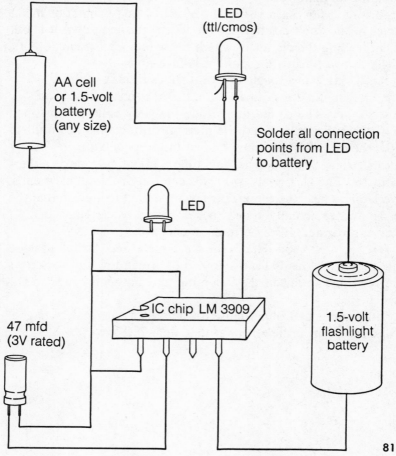

LED
(ttl/cmos)

AA cell
or 1.5-volt
battery
(any size)

Solder all connection
points from LED
to battery

LED

47 mfd
(3V rated)

IC chip LM 3909

1.5-volt
flashlight
battery

SWITCHES, SENSORS, AND DETECTORS (10 CENTS-$10)

Take an extra long look at the illustrations opposite—eight devices, only a representative collection of the hundreds of styles that are in use in security.

1. HOMEMADE. This is a simple strip of springy metal snipped from a heavy packing case. If you can locate a broken alarm clock spring, use it. Make a hole in one end (with a drill or simply by driving a small nail through it) and fasten it to a wire in a wooden window channel. When the window is raised, the tip of the spring is pressed against another wired screw, completing a circuit and sounding an alarm.

2. TOGGLE. Many fit a ¼-inch hole drilled in a cabinet or metal plate. In the "up" position it's on. When pushed down it is off, thus breaking the circuit in which it's wired. Called single-pole, single-throw. Most will require a ⅜-inch hole.

3. SLIDE. Same as a toggle except it slides instead of flips.

4. PUSH. The first push turns it on, the next push turns it off.

5. MERCURY. The connection inside the glass ball remains open until the ball is tilted and the mercury inside runs downhill to close the circuit. These can be great fun to play with.

6. GLASS/METAL REED. The glass tube is about as thick as a thermometer. The glass seals two leads entering from opposite ends, overlapping near the center. If they are manufactured so that the leads (reeds) actually touch, it's a normally closed switch. If they're separated, it's a normally open switch.

7. MAGNETIC SENSOR. Here's the glass/metal reed switch molded into plastic and ready for use in a door or window alarm. Screws are provided to fasten the incoming and outgoing wires to the switch.

8. THE MAGNET. Brought close to the sensor, the sealed magnet will close or open the sensor switch, item 7 above.

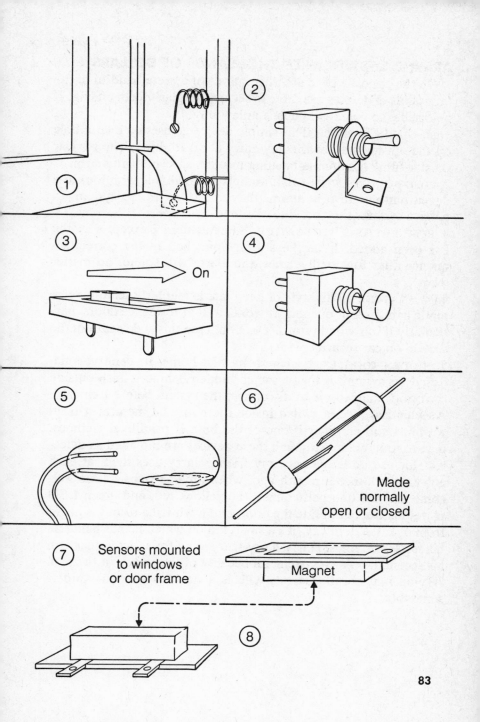

① ②

③ On

④

⑤ ⑥ Made
normally
open or closed

⑦ Sensors mounted
to windows
or door frame

Magnet

⑧

83

ARMING DEVICES (FREE–THOUSANDS OF DOLLARS)

On the opposite page are illustrations of a mere handful of the thousands of devices available to set any burglar's teeth on edge if he decides to enter a residence unlawfully.

1. SINGLE LED PLATE. This simple device is inserted over a hole on the outside wall near every entry door. It glows. The burglar must assume the double-latching mechanism works an alarm.

2. PUSH BUTTONS WITH LED. Models are available with four to a dozen buttons. In true alarms they actually arm the system. In passive systems they provide cosmetic coverage.

3. PUSH BUTTONS WITH SWITCH. Same as item 2 except a switch has been added. If the keys aren't punched in the correct sequence after four or five tries, the alarm will sound, no matter what.

4. KEY LATCHES. This style of key plate is regularly seen in automatic garage-door openers. It works well at residence doors, particularly if it is wired into LEDs. You'll see this style again in the section on car security.

5. HIDDEN TOGGLES. I secured my first home, in Pennsylvania, using this system. A toggle switch hidden behind a bush outside the house enabled me to disconnect the system before I entered. An identical hidden switch inside the house let me arm it from within. I still consider it one of the best, if primitive, methods.

6. PRESSURE PADS. Although these devices are intended as detectors for use under carpets, my friend Harry uses them at each entry door. Since a month ago, when anyone steps on his welcome mat the doorbell chimes, the yellow, red, and green LED plates light up alongside the door, and a whirring sound is heard from over the doorway (it's a small fan on which he has bent one blade). It's a typical Harry-hairy-scary. And for a fact it does arm his secondary alarm system, all because of the switch in the pad. As you may recall, Harry's wife is a nervous woman—understandably.

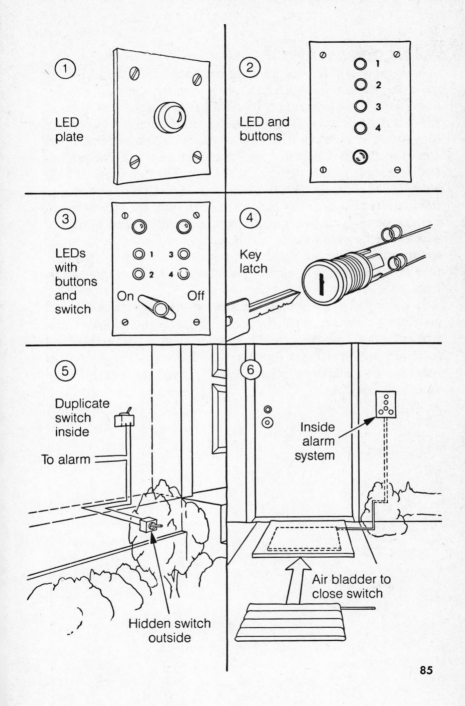

① LED plate

② LED and buttons
1
2
3
4

③ LEDs with buttons and switch
1 3
2 4
On   Off

④ Key latch

⑤ Duplicate switch inside

To alarm

Hidden switch outside

⑥ Inside alarm system

Air bladder to close switch

ALARM DEVICES: ANNUNCIATORS

As I told you at the beginning of the book, the system I use for my own residence is fundamentally a nonactive, mute, nonelectric system. In addition to my flashing LEDs and plastic foil on all windows and door latches, I maintain an unusual, probably rare item found in a junkyard. It's a monstrous electric bell that operates directly on 120 volts of alternating current. The master switch that controls it hangs near the bed. The bell itself, at least 18 inches in diameter (it's too high to measure precisely), would be instantly visible to any burglar approaching the area at night, because one of our exterior spotlights is pointed dead on it. If I encountered severe trouble within my house I wouldn't hesitate to turn that bell loose. You might install something comparable, manually operated if you don't maintain an automatic alarm system.

If nothing else, hook up some kind of manual "panic alarm." Nowadays there are expensive sirens, yelpers, and shriekers that will at least arouse the neighbors. Some samples of interior and exterior alarm devices are illustrated on the opposite page. Any of them can be made to function manually if you don't buy into an automatic control.

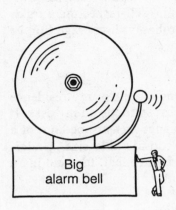

Big
alarm bell

Electronic sirens

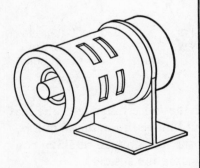

Electronic yelpers

87

LIGHTS, CAMERAS, ACTION,
AND OTHER THINGS (FREE AND OTHERWISE)

The following gadgets represent assorted arming devices, controllers, annunciators, and sensors that no self-respecting burglar would ever suspect and that would probably discourage him or her from further adventures.

Arming Devices

I arm and disarm a certain bell-ringing circuit in my residence simply by moving a small imitation Oscar statuette on my desk. It has a giant magnet in its base. The magnet was stripped out of a permanent-magnet radio speaker of considerable size. Underneath my desk top is a hinge fastened by one leaf. It's held in an "almost-closed" position by a screwnail.

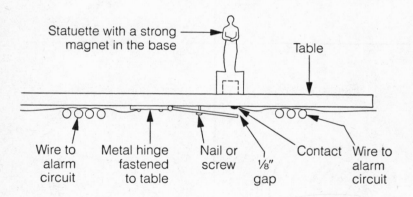

Statuette with a strong magnet in the base — Table

Wire to alarm circuit | Metal hinge fastened to table | Nail or screw | 1/8″ gap | Contact | Wire to alarm circuit

If the statuette is not directly over the loose hinge leaf, the leaf hangs and the circuit is open. When I move the statuette to a position over the hinge leaf, it clicks the leaf upward, making contact with the wired screw and activating the system.

An arming device can be as simple as a stick with a mercury switch taped to it. We have a small broken electric clock with an alarm that is frightening. We throw it in our baggage when we travel, along with a lightweight extension cord. At night I plug in the clock and prop my little knockover switch behind the door of our hotel room. If anyone enters using a passkey or a key retained from a prior occupancy, the stick is knocked over, the mercury switch is closed, the clock goes berserk, and everybody runs, I suppose. It's never been put to the test yet. This mercury-switch gimmick has dozens of applications. Use your imagination.

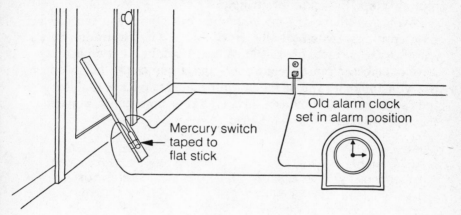

Old alarm clock
set in alarm position

Mercury switch
taped to
flat stick

Controllers

Somewhat blushingly, I admit that I can operate most toggle switches by remote control using nothing but a long piece of twine. I can turn things on or off at least once.

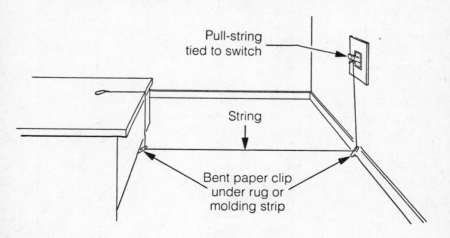

Pull-string
tied to switch

String

Bent paper clip
under rug or
molding strip

We use this trick to snap on the heater in an otherwise unheated cabin we visit occasionally out in the boondocks. I can almost always turn a distant toggle switch on or off by bending a paper clip and slipping its end over the edge of an electric cover plate, then threading the string through the clip after looping it snugly over the end of the switch toggle. Sometimes it requires a snippet of adhesive tape to secure the string.

If you don't have any mice around your home, you can use a mousetrap as a switch for all sorts of things. The illustration here shows what an incredible little gadget it can be. It is an arming device, detector/sensor, controller, and annunciator, all in one. So, with apologies and affection for the late great Rube Goldberg, here's how a 30-cent mousetrap can be your nonelectric, nonelectronic, all-inclusive burglar alarm.

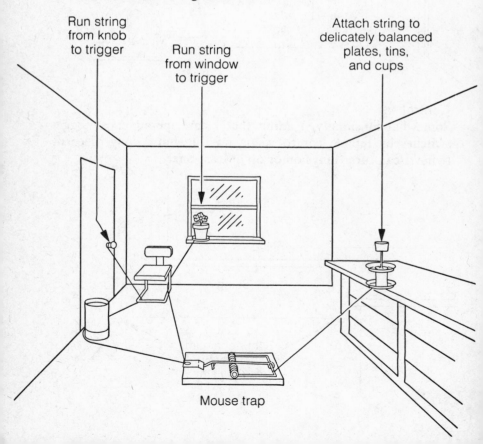

Run string from knob to trigger

Run string from window to trigger

Attach string to delicately balanced plates, tins, and cups

Mouse trap

If possible, tack or glue the trap to a solid surface. Measure off a piece of string to reach a door or window or both. Fasten one end of the string to the trigger on the trap, the other end to books or bottles that can be snuggled tight against a door or window. Measure additional string to a counter top or table. Fasten one end of the string to the heavy wire that would ordinarily dispatch the mouse. Loop the other end around artfully balanced cans and plates. Set the trap and go to bed. If the tensions on all strings have been set up carefully, any movement at a door or window will trigger the trap, causing the heavy bar to snap over, tightening the string and toppling your carefully balanced stack of noisemakers. It could produce enough racket to send the burglar running.

Rat traps will scare off bigger rats. And if you plan thoughtfully you can rig this system to be on the alert inside your residence even while you're away—you set it gently, step over the threshold, and close your door. The trap can be rigged as an electric contact, photo flasher, all sorts of things. And the mice will thank you for getting off their backs.

Fire and Smoke Alarms

Whether they are fire and heat sensors or smoke detectors, they can be set up to function on their own or as parts of a total household, apartment, or office system.

Smoke sensors come in two basic types, and they are not worth the effort of trying to manufacture them on a kitchen table. The photoelectric types employ a complicated chamber that excludes outside light but admits outside air. A minuscule beam of light is aimed at a photoelectric cell. If smoke enters the space, its particles diffuse the light, which causes the circuit to close and activate an alarm.

The ionization types require a minuscule amount of radioactive material, which ionizes the air within an inner chamber. If smoke enters the chamber, the ionized air becomes conductive and sounds the alarm.

Increasingly, nationwide, smoke and fire detectors are required by law for installation in every hotel and apartment dwelling. But then what? Will people react appropriately after they've been alerted to smoke or fire dangers? Our family faces up seriously to regular fire drills, no embarrassment, no foolishness. We do a little drill. Then we have a party. By the way, an average smoke/fire detector costs $10–$15.

Heat and fire alarms, like smoke detectors, are really nothing more than normally open switches. Sensors can readily be wired into any burglar-alarm system that accepts N.O. circuits. I've made a dozen or more from old choke springs from carburetors. These are bimetal coils that expand when heated. I hook one wire to the spring, the other wire to a screw that I position experimentally by heating the coil with a match. When the spring touches the screw, the circuit is closed. In a controller it would activate an alarm. In my son's home I've got two of the choke-spring gadgets wired to monitor the dampers in his fireplace and the temperature of the flue on his wood-burning stove. Many other possibilities.

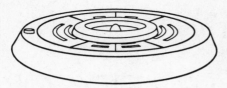

$10–$15
Standard smoke
fire alarm. 9-volt
battery needed.

CAUTION! As smoke rises, it
tends to veer away from walls
near ceiling. Your detector
should be mounted at least
18″ from ceiling.

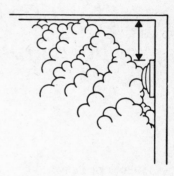

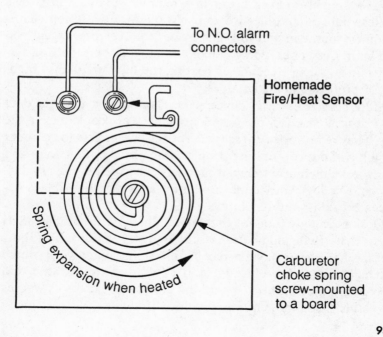

To N.O. alarm
connectors

**Homemade
Fire/Heat Sensor**

Spring expansion when heated

Carburetor
choke spring
screw-mounted
to a board

6

SECURITY FOR PROPERTY INSIDE AND OUTSIDE YOUR HOME

As mentioned several times in this book, security devices overlap in their purposes and locations. Items that work well in your windows might do even better in a relative's doors. Again, let's not lose sight of our objective: to push you toward a system that is uniquely your own and full of surprises for everyone except you and your loved ones. Being one of a kind, your personalized system stands a better chance of beating the burglars than a high-priced professional system does.

More burglaries of residences take place during daylight than after dark. Reason? More homes are empty of people during the day. They're at work or at school. The burglar prefers to go about his job without confronting people. If he observes that John and Mary leave their apartment at precisely the same time every day, it would be logical for him to plan his attack on their place between breakfast and lunchtime.

Dusk is an ugly time for burglaries. There's a lot of tension as folks start arriving home from work, tired and anxious. If the burglar has had a slow day, he may be forced into night work, which will make him or her a bit edgy, too. (You're aware, I'm sure, that women are moving heavily into the burglary business as well as into other fields formerly the province of men.)

Once darkness settles in, things seem to settle down again until the real professional midnight burglars start prowling. They are nowhere near as numerous, but they have incredible skills compared to most of the daylight thieves. They delight in entering a residence, cleaning it out of valuables, and leaving while the owners are asleep. Usually they'll do anything to avoid face-to-face confrontation, but if the pressure is really on them, they'll fight back, often with tragic results for the homeowner.

The only other thing we should remember has to do with geography. In the small oceanside community where I reside there are plenty of burglaries, but most of the burglars are juveniles or amateurs. The big-timers work the known affluent districts farther inland.

Parts of Los Angeles, like parts of New York, Chicago, and other major metropolitan areas, seem to be infested with a disproportionate number of gang thieves and crazies. Sickies. New York has some special problems, such as its subways, which increase the personal-threat factor and give thieves additional escape routes.

EXTERIORS

Whether it's an apartment in New York or a small ranch in the Phoenix area, I will always insist on plenty of lights to start coming on strong as soon as the sun starts to fade around my home area. The illustration opposite won't be too helpful to most apartment dwellers, though it should provide some ideas. Actually, that drawing is an approximation of my son's alarm system, the one he started installing and has been adding to ever since his stripped-to-the-walls burglary last year. Only weeks ago he added some concealed pressure pads that chime out if an intruder gets close to windows and doors. The initial timer and a couple of floodlights plus new locks, totaled approximately $150. Then he started shopping and came up with secondhand components, exterior conduits, even floodlights. Where he could find decent weather protection he used some hideaway timers picked up on sale at drugstores. They are intended for interior use, but he already has a houseful of timers ticking inside and he fully intends to replace the cheapie items with heavy-duty exterior timers as he finds them. Recently at a house-wrecking yard he purchased ten fire detectors and six smoke alarms, complete, for $5.

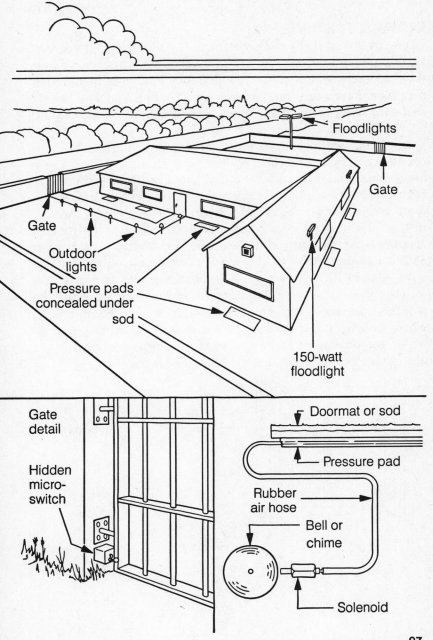

Floodlights

Gate

Gate

Outdoor lights

Pressure pads concealed under sod

150-watt floodlight

Gate detail

Hidden micro-switch

Doormat or sod

Pressure pad

Rubber air hose

Bell or chime

Solenoid

EXTERIOR SURPRISES

The front and rear patios of a townhouse we lease are guarded night and day at no cost by an impressive army of cactus plants that become a beautiful garden when they burst into bloom. Our neighbors have been burglarized. We have not. Dare we believe that our residence was cased by the same burglars and rejected? If so, were the cactus plants the reason?

My friend and colleague Berni resides in a house that is surrounded by an impenetrable 10-foot vine. He never thought of it as a burglary defense until we found ourselves talking about it in terms of this book one day, months and months ago. He was so impressed that he already has the vine growing wildly through the bars of the single wide gate with a double latch that gives him access to the garden and house. He has removed a burglar alarm/announcer that was installed when the house was built. It once worked by air pressure. A rubber bag, not unlike a hot-water bottle, was squeezed when a visitor stepped onto the planked area under the gate. The air was compressed up a pipe, where a tiny plunger was forced out to strike a chime. He converted the pneumatic feature to an electric one, as shown in the illustration below. But either system would work.

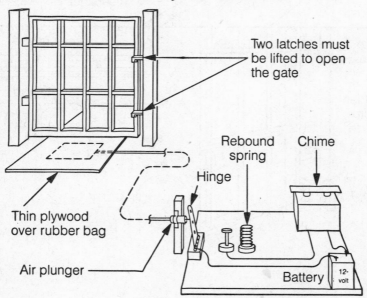

Two latches must be lifted to open the gate

Rebound spring

Chime

Hinge

Thin plywood over rubber bag

Air plunger

Battery

12-volt

TAPE-RECORDER WATCHMAN

Any old or new cassette tape player can be rigged to deliver a message to any invader of your house. It can even be adapted to alert a nearby household by simply plugging in the extension speaker.

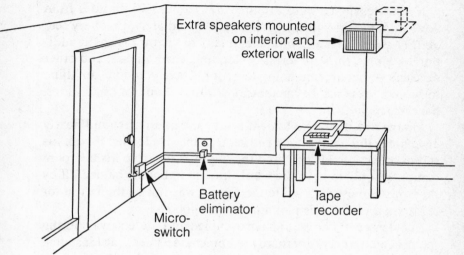

Extra speakers mounted on interior and exterior walls

Battery eliminator

Micro-switch

Tape recorder

This is the alarm machine protecting these premises. Your presence here has been noted. The family's security system has been dialed and the police have been called to [give address]. You have been warned.

Repeat such a message several times—at least ten times.

To activate the machine, the simplest technique is to fasten a microswitch to any part of the doorframe so that it will close and activate a battery eliminator, which in turn will begin to feed the tape machine. Unplug the battery eliminator to shut down the system.

Old, junked telephone-answering machines are easily purchased for $5 or less in many junk shops and repair outlets. They work ideally for such purposes if in fact there is not going to be any automatic dial-out.

HIGH-PRIORITY ITEMS

Okay, now comes the tough stuff. Other than your family and pets, what are the items most precious to you? The key word that might help you is *irreplaceable*. Family photos? Birth certificates? Personal letters? Other vital documents?

If your residence were to burst into flames five minutes from now, what would you start collecting immediately, that very second? (Assume that all living creatures are secure.) Also, in addition to flames, think in terms of flooding, earthquakes, and other disasters. What are you going to go for? Have you done anything to protect these priority possessions from calamities of all kinds, burglary included?

I know one man who bought a safe at a swap meet and nearly gave himself a heart attack getting it home. He loaded it with his stamp collection, his will, and the floppy disks from his bedroom computer, only to have the whole kit and kaboodle hauled off by brigands one evening while the family was out of the house for less than an hour. His planning wasn't good.

In at least eight houses I have occupied and traded away during the past quarter century there are homemade safes that I installed in the floors and walls, mostly in the basements. I make the safes of 6-inch-diameter casing pipe, like sewer pipe, usually cut 24 inches long. I have a plumber caulk a cleanout plug into one end, and I have a mild steel plate brazed onto the other end. If you use cast-iron pipe, remember, it cannot be welded. It can be brazed, however. I hammer a hole in the concrete-block walls, dig out enough earth to insert my safe, and cement it into place. It looks like a plumbing outlet, but it's full of my few valuables. The safe itself is lined with felt. I open and close it with a big adjustable wrench. It works!

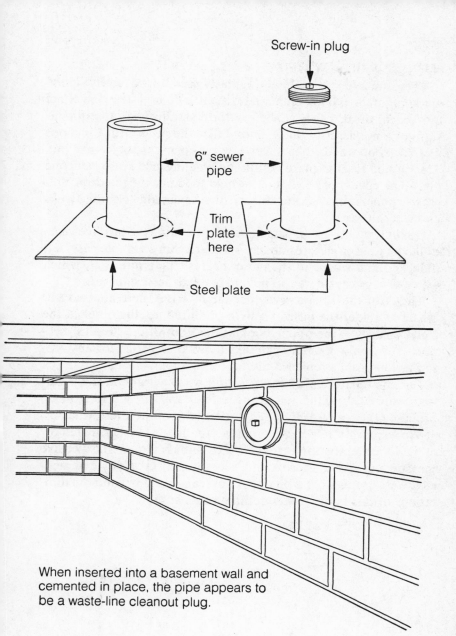

Screw-in plug

6″ sewer pipe

Trim plate here

Steel plate

When inserted into a basement wall and cemented in place, the pipe appears to be a waste-line cleanout plug.

MEDIUM-PRIORITY ITEMS

There are a few good things regularly used by the family. These are kept safe in a book on a library shelf. The first step is to select a practical tin box that is about a third smaller than the dimensions of a nondescript book. Immobilize the book with C-clamps and strips of wood, then saber-saw or razor-cut the center out. The tin box is set in place within the hole, fastened in by silicone glue. The covers of the book are held together by glued-on Velcro® fasteners, in case any future thieves should toss the books about recklessly.

Our current, in-use papers of value, including the last five years of income-tax copies, reside in a standard thin steel tote case, left unlocked and stored in the closet nearest the main door, which we've always considered to be our best exit in case of a fire.

Then, for the emergencies that might arise, there are two $10 bills, one under the base of a living-room lamp, the other in the Yellow Pages of the phone book at the front of the "Banks" section. Any family member can take a bill at any time for any reason as long as it's replaced the following day.

For emergency use of another kind we generally have a 5-gallon bottle of drinking water and a few cans of food in storage, probably the result of living in earthquake-prone California.

We've never found need to rent a safe-deposit box or feared for a world calamity tomorrow. We've simply taken inexpensive measures to provide for routine security and everyday emergencies. Catastrophes are a bit out of our league and beyond the limitations of this book, to say nothing of its author.

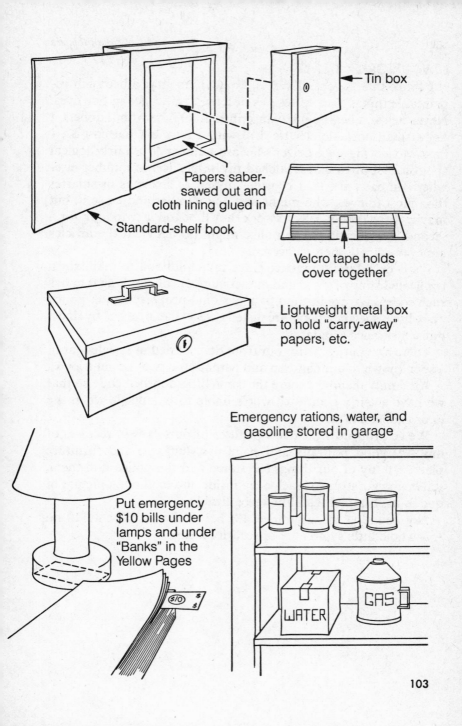

Tin box

Papers saber-sawed out and cloth lining glued in

Standard-shelf book

Velcro tape holds cover together

Lightweight metal box to hold "carry-away" papers, etc.

Emergency rations, water, and gasoline stored in garage

Put emergency $10 bills under lamps and under "Banks" in the Yellow Pages

$10
$
$

WATER

GAS

LOW-PRIORITY ITEMS

I think that stereos, TV sets, typewriters, and other such re-placeable things are possessions of least significance in our lives. Nevertheless, I begrudgingly inscribed all of ours with numbers. I use a small portable electric drill with a burr bit that cost $2. I have etched my own driver's-license number in a fairly logical spot on each item and scratched my wife's license number else-where on each article. I consider myself as smart as or smarter than most thieves, who might find one number and erase it, but maybe if they're too lazy to work they'll be too lazy to look for a second identification. The police might do better, if the articles are ever swiped, then recovered.

It's been a family practice since my childhood to maintain a triplicate listing of serial and model numbers of anything that has such codes. We are insured by a personal-property floater policy on which specific items are listed—very inexpensive by most other insurance standards.

There are spare keys for our front door buried in a sealed jar in a spot known to our children and parents and two special friends.

All family members share the same little doorbell code so that we have a fairly good idea who's liable to be outside when the door gadget chirps.

We've dropped wallet-size pictures of ourselves in recesses of our few good portraits and paintings, luggage, and furniture pieces. If any of our things are stolen and the police find them, it'll be invigorating to reach deep inside and haul out a picture of one of us. I hope I'll still be recognizable.

Not counting the insurance, I'll bet we haven't spent $10 on this whole little symphony of security ideas.

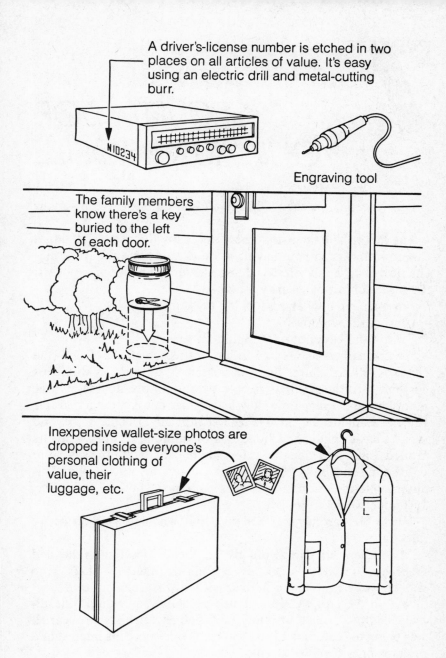

A driver's-license number is etched in two places on all articles of value. It's easy using an electric drill and metal-cutting burr.

Engraving tool

The family members know there's a key buried to the left of each door.

Inexpensive wallet-size photos are dropped inside everyone's personal clothing of value, their luggage, etc.

7

SECURITY FOR YOUR AUTOMOBILE

People frequently say, "Oh, I don't know a blasted thing about cars."

The fact is, of course, that there are many things an individual can do with cars without having to know word one about the mechanical, hydraulic, electrical, or vacuum functioning of cars. Take the subject of security for cars.

For openers, how about locking the doors?

Closing the windows?

Taking the keys out of the ignition?

An uncle of mine, George Elliott, retired chief of police of the city of Toronto, claims that the volume of auto thefts would be cut by more than half if people would simply do these three humble things every time they leave their autos unattended. He will not estimate the savings such action might achieve, beyond suggesting it could total hundreds of millions of dollars in the United States and Canada. "How about calculating the saving of police time and skills for important things?" my uncle says. "This automobile-theft nonsense is a big pain in the neck to the police. Just paperwork. Stupidity."

Uncle George never talked like that when he was on active duty.

My father did. He swore by all the deities that if he had George's job, he'd lock up any idiotic blankety-blank who walked away from his or her car without first locking it.

Within the past week I watched a young man sign an installment contract for an uncanny theft gadget for his sports car. It was going to cost him at least $600 plus sales tax plus interest and perhaps fines for false alarms.

In my opinion, 't'ain't worth it.

Yet the theft of your automobile represents a series of shocks and inconveniences: the momentary panic on discovering your auto missing; the disbelief that some rascal must have stolen it; the scuttering around for owner's documents; the tensions of police and insurance interviews; the discomfort of borrowing or renting a strange car; the daily wait for a report on your car's recapture; the mixed feelings about getting it back. Will the engine be ruined? Will the interior be stripped? Befouled?

No matter what, it's a rotten experience.

I will propose to you a succession of steps you can undertake by yourself to make your car reasonably theftproof. Skip any or all the steps you don't like, can't afford, or consider unworthy. Install all and you'll have a few extra switches to snap when arming or disarming your car. You'll have to judge for yourself.

A STEPPED PROCEDURE FOR VEHICLE PROTECTION

We'll describe an orderly procedure for adding cosmetic and active devices that will be applicable to most automobiles. Depending on your choices of gadgets, your tool requirements may include an electric drill with metal cutters, pliers, soldering iron, solder, flux, vinyl tape, a handful of wrenches, and a healthy supply of electric wire designed for auto use, preferably 14 gauge or better. You'll find the parts you need at auto supply shops, junkyards, or through mail-order companies such as Whitney's, P.O. Box 8410, Chicago IL 60680.

Before you start, reexamine the prior material on items like the LED flasher (page 80) and the switches (page 82). This time around think of them in terms of their applications to your car.

STEP 1. IGNITION DISCONNECTOR. Buy one or several toggle switches, preferably of the ¼-inch-mount type, with screw fasteners. You want a switch that'll slip into a hole of a size for which you have a drill—so think ahead. Drill a hole in the fire wall or dashboard area, probably within reach, but obscure. Run two wires through the hole in which you've installed a grommet or insulated liner.

STEP 2. PREPARING THE SWITCH. Locate the single thin wire that runs from your distributor to one of the two small connectors on the coil. It'll probably be designated with a minus sign. Unfasten that wire and in its place fasten one of the two wires from your toggle switch. Then solder the disconnected "primary" wire to the other wire from your toggle switch. Thread the wiring (called dressing the wires) carefully, away from superhot engine parts. Now your ignition key will not start the engine until the switch is flicked to the "on" position. This system isn't practical for diesel or positive-grounded cars.

STEP 3. MASTER BATTERY DISCONNECT. Your local auto-parts store may stock an $8 master switch (Whitney's #15-0856Y is $8.50) that can be mounted under the dash or hood with cables running to and from the big, main battery. It's a big and husky switch, too. It can shut down *everything* when you leave your car and switch to "off." You must plan carefully to fasten the wires so

Step 1

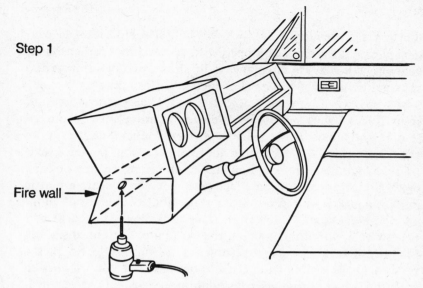

Fire wall →

In a concealed area of the fire wall, drill a hole large enough to accomodate a rubber grommet and 2 wires.

Step 2

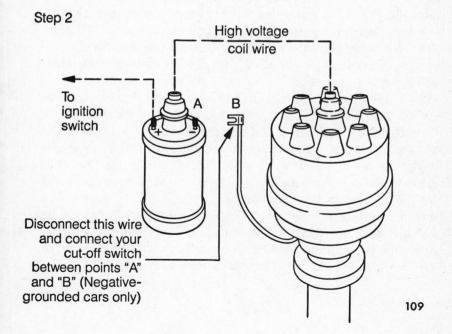

High voltage coil wire

To ignition switch

A   B

Disconnect this wire and connect your cut-off switch between points "A" and "B" (Negative-grounded cars only)

109

that any electric alarms or clock will be left energized. And *caution, please:* If the car is equipped with an alternator rather than a generator, the engine must always be shut down before you disconnect the battery by means of such a big switch.

STEP 4. COSMETIC KEY SWITCH AND LABEL. Classy auto stores and some Radio Shack outlets sell a clever $2 imitation keyhole assembly and a reasonably scary "WARNING" label that are simply adhesive-pressed into place to a door panel or front fender. I realize I downgraded printed, phony labels much earlier, but, on cars, these gimmicks seem to be effective. If you can't locate a plastic imitation, ask your locksmith or garage-door people for an inoperable garage-door switch from their junk box. Then drill and ream a hole in the side panel of the car fender or door, installing the broken switch by its screw-down nut, from inside. So, pick a position that's visible from outside but easy for you to work at from the inside during your installation. It is usually easiest near the front-door hinge on the driver's side.

STEP 5. MOTION DETECTOR. The device illustrated retails from $2 to $8 and is readily installed under the hood, anywhere near the horn relay. The thing is little more than a pendulum that swings, contacts electrically with the horn and toots relentlessly if the car is jiggled more than the sensitivity control permits. (Whitney's catalog number is 88-7196U; $2.98.) On all store-bought items you'll get lots of installation instructions. So, keep cool.

STEP 6. HOOD SWITCH. If you already have a light that glows when the car hood is lifted, consider adding a scrap of extension wire from the line that feeds the bulb to the positive input side of the horn relay. Again, wire into another toggle switch so that you can have the oil checked without sounding the alarm. Another scheme is to mount a mercury switch on or within one of the hood brackets, same method as Step 2. If the hood is raised for a naughty purpose the mercury will swirl around the contact points and the horn will blast. These switches have multiple applications. They are sometimes held in place best with string, putty, or the metal body-patching compounds such as Bondo®.

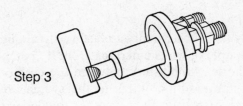

Step 3

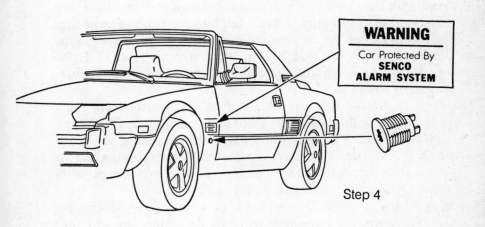

WARNING

Car Protected By
**SENCO
ALARM SYSTEM**

Step 4

Step 5

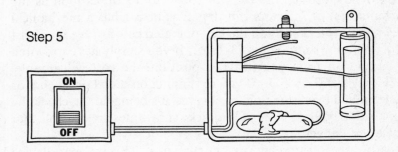

ON

OFF

STEP 7. SEAT SWITCH. This is usually a plastic strip about 8 inches in length with a couple of wires emerging from it. You need simply slide it into the seat upholstery between the cushioning and the driver's personal padding. Wires to the switch are usually threaded under the carpeting up to another toggle switch—yes, still another one under the dashboard or wherever you have selected to squirrel such things. One wire to the power supply, the second to a horn relay or some other 12-volt noisemaker. Personally, I prefer hooking into another, second, miniature lantern battery. In the beginning, you'll sound the alarm every time you sit in your car. But quickly you'll fall into the habit of switching the seat switch off before sitting down. Ask any security store for this item, usually less than $5. An alternative is a piece of Tapeswitch®, which is a similar type of pressure switch, sold like carpeting, by the yard.

STEP 8. IGNITION CUTOFF. This gadget, when turned on, stalls your engine within 20 to 30 seconds of operation. (Whitney's #14-2193N; $20.) Or try your local store. The thing just hides under the dash or in the glove compartment, hooked up with two wires. Makes a car impervious to "hot-wiring," which represents a nice little bonus, don't you think?

STEP 9. FUEL CUTOFFS. If your car is now equipped with an electric fuel pump, you have it made. Hook the connecting wire into another cheap toggle switch. Some pumps will have two wires running to them; most have only one. With the switch interrupting the flow of fuel, the car will cough to a stop as soon as the carburetor(s) or injectors run dry. If your car has a mechanical fuel pump, you can install the key-operated cutoff valve for about $20. (Whitney's number is 73-2875.) If you simply have to switch it on and off from your driver's position, the cost will double. (Whitney's #73-5049U.) If you're running on diesel or alcohol or fuel distilled from week-old bread (yes, it's being done), check the application before buying. Gimmicky substitutes are possible, but much too dangerous.

STEP 10. MECHANICAL BRAKE/WHEEL LOCK. This two-part device clips over the steering wheel and under the brake pedal and locks,

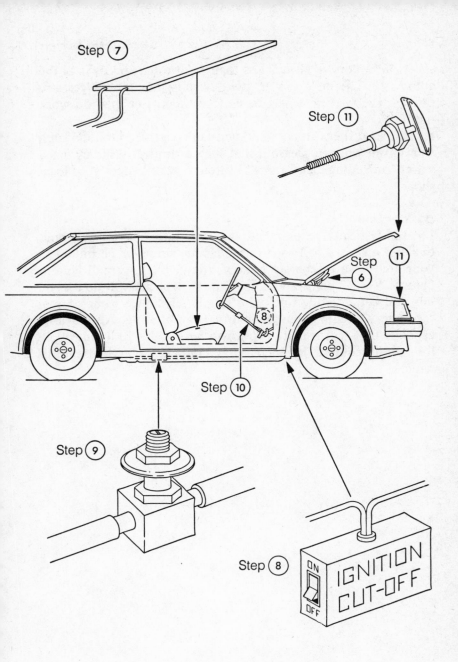

Step ⑦

Step ⑪

Step
⑥

⑪

⑧

Step ⑩

Step ⑨

Step ⑧

ON
OFF

IGNITION
CUT-OFF

click, click. They're always less than $10 on bargain days at the auto store. The only flaw in the device is that car thieves saw through the steering wheel to remove them. But they do work nicely.

STEP 11. LATCHES AND LOCKS. If you can't control your hood latch from inside the car, please install such a control. Whitney has a variety, including locks, from $5 through $25. So does your local shop.

Bottom Line

I enthusiastically recommend that you think seriously about hooking up extra bells, whistles, yelpers, sirens (if permitted in your area) into a separate battery circuit. Even a small lantern battery, 6 or 12 volts, about 1.5 ampere capacity will do a good job. It'll befuddle the thief who simply clips away your normal car-battery circuitry, but the alarms stay blasting. Also, a low-capacity unit will usually run down within the 10-minute time limitation required by increasing numbers of antinoise ordinances.

# PERSONAL SECURITY

C'mon, step outside with me. Let's go strolling!

There are a few but only a few places in this great Northern Hemisphere where I'd be unwilling to go out walking at any time of the night or day. I'm certain that if I were a woman my list of dangerous territories would be longer, but only until I'd completed a basic course in self-defense tactics. I refer here not to the mystic Eastern arts but rather to the new programs that teach students to break arms, snap legs, gouge eyes, and in general drop any attacker to the ground, senseless—zip, zap, whap! I have enrolled in such a program.

SAD BUT TRUE, BUT LIMITED

There were 3,140 murders committed during 1981 in the state of California, cited here only because it's the biggest state, with the most dramatic crime coverage. That's a lot of murdering. That's more than 260 individuals per month, 8 per day, falling victim to the ultimate violence. It's horrifying as a statistic and a dreadful commentary on our society. But let's not be terrorized by it. Among 25 million people it represents one murder per 8,000 individuals.

Significantly, two of every three murder victims had had a long personal relationship with their attacker. In actual fact, only one murder of every five proves to be the result of a confrontation between total strangers. Guns account for 60 percent of the killings. Other weapons or bodily assaults account for the remainder.

Always mindful of the tragic potentials, I cling to the belief that if I lead a fairly prudent life in a reasonably civil community, my chances of falling victim to a heinous crime are very remote. While it is impossible to maintain a perfect defense against the crazies in our society, the odds of being killed in an auto accident are ten times greater than of being killed an by unknown sickie.

Nevertheless, we must cope with that small percentage of individuals and circumstances that would deprive us of our possessions or cause us bodily harm while we're at work, at home, or walking through any neighborhood. There are some logical and positive things we can do to outwit attackers and robbers.

CARDS AND DOCUMENTS (FREE–$10)

Because I persisted through a couple of years of friendly persuasion, every member of the family now maintains a regularly updated list of all the numbers and data pertinent to our credit cards, bank accounts, and other documents. Each of us has a bureau tray into which the day's receipts, bills, reminder notes, and other clutter are tossed. Usually twice each month, or when the spirit moves us, the debris is pawed over, sorted out, and arranged for check writing, filing, or discarding. It's always a good feeling when I see the box on my end of the dressing table empty. Whenever numbers must be changed, they're processed on the spot. It has been a personal preference with us, but we do not subscribe to any central services that maintain lists of our credit cards and other documents. We consider such organizations to represent another invasion of our personal privacy. We cherish what little remains of that privacy. Perhaps I'm fanatic, but I don't give away things like my Social Security number without first knowing the reasons why it may be needed by others. Social Security was never intended to be an identification card. Bankers, the IRS, and politicians encourage this perversion, regrettably.

Most of us in the family (not all) carry two wallets at all times. The "stealing" wallet contains some expired credit cards and a few single dollars. That's the one to be handed over to anyone who says, "Holdup." The real wallet with the current cards, documents, and photocopies of precious belongings is tucked away in an inside pocket or in the belt purse. The illustration should indicate how easy it would be to make one if you can't find one at your store. It's little more than a rectangle of light leather, folded to a flap, punched, and threaded with a thong.

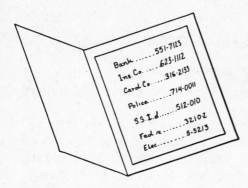

An updated listing of all cards and documents showing numbers to be called in event of theft or loss. Kept in safe, "tin box," and on writing desk.

The "Stealing" Wallet

Holds expired credit cards and four single dollar bills

Real Wallet

This one contains the current cards and cash

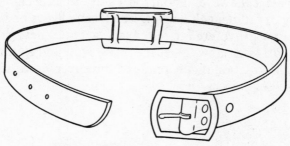

Favorite Wallet
(On belt)

EMERGENCY FUNDS AND PROTECTORS
(FREE–$25)

Can you picture yourself being robbed, left penniless and abandoned, almost anywhere? Think about it. Then protect against it.

A dear friend prodded me into the habit of always carrying, concealed, a dime, a quarter, and one large denomination of paper money, somewhere on my clothing. I discovered I could slit open the lining of a couple of my belts to conceal paper money. I've got quarters glued behind the buckles of some other belts. When men's hats were in vogue I hid money in sandwich bags in the bands and/or decorations. The ladies in the family have taken to the same miniature plastic bags, which they pin near waistbands and zippers, inside their dresses or slacks. My mother is alleged to always have a $20 bill in her bosom, which she refers to as the "home bank." She rarely carries a handbag anymore. "Too damned old-fashioned," says this hyper octogenarian.

In certain states of America and provinces of Canada it's permissible to tote canisters of mace, a tear-gas type of substance available in pressurized canisters. I don't like the stuff. Improperly used, it can permanently damage the eyes or respiratory systems of both the attacker and attackee. I keep hearing from the experts that by the time the owner has fished the can of gas out of his or her pocket or purse, it's too late to use it anyway. If I felt I should carry mace, however, and if local authorities declared it to be legal, I'd carry it in a belt holster, which can always be bought with the canisters. If you're interested, contact your nearest security company to learn how to get the awful stuff and sign up for the course of instruction that is required for buyer/users of mace and other aerosol devices.

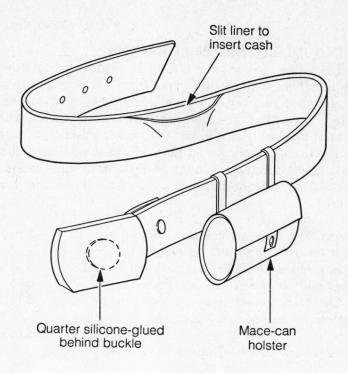

Slit liner to
insert cash

Quarter silicone-glued
behind buckle

Mace-can
holster

SECURITY SUNDRIES (ALL PRICE RANGES)

Friend Hellman likes security alarms as a career because they can stop hoodlums without destroying them. He is one of those people who shoo flies out the front door rather than swatting them. He believes that life is too precious to be tampered with, regardless of its intelligence level. After much pushing, though, he took me to his suppliers and pointed out the hottest-selling items, all of them effective, although he deplores the life-threatening ones. Six of the profit-makers are illustrated. Prices are retail in mid-1983.

1. Chem Lite®. A flashlight that also sprays gas.	$30
2. Sock It Away®. A polyester stocking/pocket pair.	$ 8
3. Tear gas. Mace. Overkill in a can. Permit needed.	$ 6
4. Paper Tiger®. It detects counterfeit currency!	$80
5. Billy Club®. Loaded with tear gas. Get an okay.	$30
6. Touch alarm, door hanger. Touch door, it screams.	$15 up
7. Counter Attack®. High-voltage shocker. Dangerous.	$35

Currently, they are big sale items.

Hellman lists dozens of others, among them: Shriek Alert®, our old friend the Freon horn blaster, $6; Repulse®, a can of hideously foul-smelling harmless gas, $6; alcohol test—several types to reveal your own or others' blood-alcohol levels (good for one's self-discipline), $80; Paralyzer®, tear-gas canister on a key ring (get training), $20; drawer alarm, several types for many purposes—in a cashbox it'll activate alarms if the bottom bill is removed, $90.

Take another look at that last item. Think how easy it would be to get a wired clothespin and make a trip pull, a piece of plastic that can be flipped out from the contacts to sound the alarm. General Supply (page 135) has all this paraphernalia, if you want any.

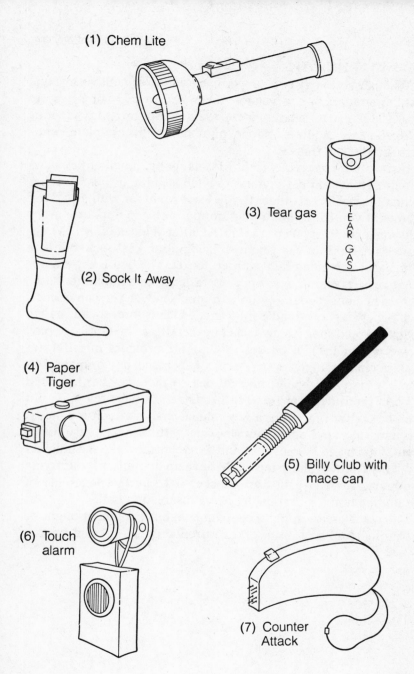

(1) Chem Lite

(3) Tear gas

(2) Sock It Away

(4) Paper Tiger

(5) Billy Club with mace can

(6) Touch alarm

(7) Counter Attack

KEYS AND HOLDERS

Whether you carry two, ten, or twenty keys around with you is less important than how you tote them. Are yours on one gigantic ring? I urge you to separate them. (And do not carry any identification—name, address, phone number, or license-plate number—on the key rings.)

First of all, the great weight of a dangling, jangling key mass hanging from your car's ignition switch is going to wear out that switch long before its time. If you leave your car with a parking attendant you hand him a grand opportunity to duplicate every key you own. In my own case, at last, after years of effort, I've acquired the habit of carrying a single ignition key on a split ring and plastic fob in my right trouser pocket. The house key and related keys travel in my left pocket, fastened to a miniature flashlight. The hodgepodge keys, plus a mini-screwdriver, can opener, and paper snip, overload a split ring, which is forever causing me to get rips and snags in my jacket pocket. It's a small price to pay, however, for the advantages this jumble provides me. If I am walking in a strange area or dark, lonely place, day or night, I fit the key ring and holder into my fist so that the sharp pointed objects protrude from between my fingers. I have felt silly, but unashamed in practicing a few maneuvers, alone, in my study, gripping the keys and shadowboxing with an imaginary opponent. I duck and dodge, twist and weave, meanwhile slashing out with my fistful of sharp metal. I'd have no hesitation about trying to defend myself against an attacker if I saw the possibility of wounding him (or her) before being disabled myself.

It's not a pretty thing to contemplate, but perhaps it might be helpful should any distasteful confrontation be pressed on me.

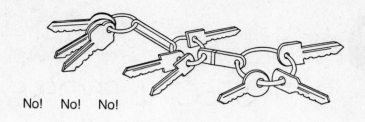

No! No! No!

Car ignition/door key

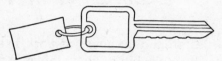

House, trunk,
garage keys, and
tiny flashlight

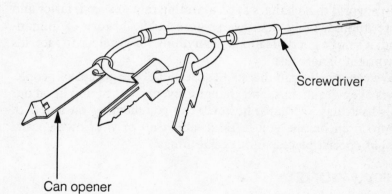

Screwdriver

Can opener

SPECIAL PEOPLE, SPECIAL PLACES, SPECIAL THINGS

In our everyday activities, around the house, at work, in school, at play, most of us fall easily into habits of doing things in routine ways, sometimes good, sometimes otherwise. We take many things for granted. The lights will always go on when we push a button. The elevator will not move until the doors are fully closed. Old man Potts might act a bit queer at times, but he's probably harmless. Et cetera. Et cetera.

In a world that changes at an alarming rate of speed, faster and more unpredictably than ever before in the history of humankind, it's not a good idea to take anything for granted. In fact, it's downright dangerous.

We cannot cover in this small space all of the groups of people, types of environments, and changing events that thump upon our lives each day. Perhaps, however, by commenting on a few of them I'll encourage you to think about all of your own special people, special places, and special things.

SPECIAL PEOPLE
Females
One of the things that makes women a special group, particularly as targets for criminality, is their inherently weaker physical strength. Men routinely beat up women more frequently than they punch out other males. Women's costumes, especially their footwear, make them extra vulnerable to attack because most of them can't run from trouble as fast as men can.

Children

Children, virtually from infancy, are the objects of criminality probably more heinous than the routine felonies perpetrated against adults. The lifetime effects of crimes against them are incalculable. Three-, four- and five-year-olds are being engaged in pornographic movie making. Increasing numbers of infants are bashed dead. Our little people are being molested by their parents, other relatives, neighbors, doctors, dentists, baby sitters! So, what can we do about it? We can't hover over the children every minute of the day and night. No, rather, let's trust them. Let's do the equivalent of drilling out a child's-eye inspection port in the front door and let them know what they're up against. Let them see what could happen. From a mountain of material I've collected I picked out ten rules that just might work if driven consistently into the mind of our own special child among all our special children.

Dear son, dear daughter, dear child:

1. Always go straight to school and return the same way.
2. Walk always with companions or authorized adults.
3. Never play around strange locations, no matter how attractive.
4. Play only in supervised areas where you know you'll be safe.
5. Never allow any stranger to touch you, no matter what reason he or she might give, unless your parents are present, as at the doctor's. Other than your parents or grandparents, who may help you wash and dress, never allow any adults to touch your private parts for any reason.
6. Never, but never, enter a school washroom or public lavatory unless you are accompanied by a trusted friend, an authorized monitor, or an adult who is well known to you and your parents.
7. If ever you are greeted by a stranger, do not respond. Instead, run full speed to your home or school, a bank, or store. If the stranger speaks to you from an automobile, try to remember the license-plate number of the car and report it, as fast as you can, to the nearest parent or authority.

8. Realize now and always believe that a police officer is your friend, someone you should not fear or ignore.
9. Memorize the location of homes in your neighborhood where you know you can always run for safety.
10. Ask one or both of your parents to walk along to school with you from time to time. Ask them to point out anything you might be doing wrong. Talk about any people or places that might not be safe for you, places like gang hangouts on street corners, dark alleys, and abandoned buildings. Learn to talk to your parents so they will learn how to talk to you.

Seniors

I'd been lounging around the police station waiting for an interview with one of their specialists when a young officer entered the receiving area pushing a teenager ahead of him, somewhat roughly I thought.

"That was a juvenile who ambushed a senior citizen who'd just cashed his Social Security check," my host said later. "All of us here, I guess every cop everywhere, gets a bit uptight around the third and fourth of each month when Social Security checks go out."

When people reach Social Security age, physical and mental reflexes tend to slacken off. I knew it for a fact when I saw my own parents endorsing their checks before leaving the house to cash them at the bank. They could have been ripped off before cashing those checks or after they'd been changed into currency. Now, finally, I've talked my parents into having their checks deposited automatically in their checking accounts, direct, by computer. It's a service anyone in the system can have for the asking and it seems to work exceedingly well. Of course, anyone whose physical strength is impaired or waning should be particularly attentive to security measures.

SPECIAL PLACES
Hotel Rooms

Earlier when we treated the subject of the fall-down mercury switch, reference was made to the vulnerability of the hotel-room guest. The hundreds or thousands of previous room users include those who held on to their keys. A few years ago when my work required me to travel a great deal, I invested in the now-famous travel lock gadget, pictured here.

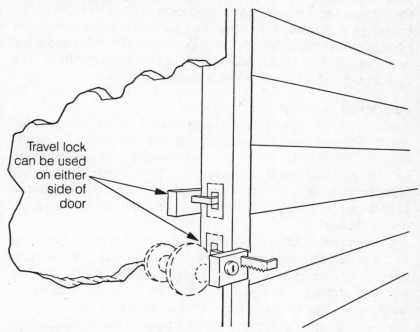

Travel lock can be used on either side of door

When snapped into position inside the door, nobody, but nobody, can get into the room with a passkey or unreturned door key. Reversed, when leaving the room, the lock makes it impossible for anyone, including the housekeeper, to enter. It's a good idea to coordinate one's use of the travellock with the bedmakers.

Also, for what it may be worth to you, I personally shun high-level room assignments. My brother-in-law stows a thin, knotted poly-plastic rope that he could readily fasten and use to descend seven or eight stories in the event of a major hotel fire. The hundred feet of rope takes up little more space than a bathrobe in his luggage. I haven't gone that route myself but be assured that I know the location of every staircase, exit, and fire-equipment box within minutes of checking into my room, anywhere.

Transportation Stops

Citizens of any metropolitan area can group together into watch patrols to assist professional agencies and can also lobby for improved security in transportation systems. Individual travelers should wait for their public transportation in brightly lighted, patrolled areas. Subway riders traveling particularly late at night or early in the morning will want to stick close to the train conductor or a transit patrol officer. All mass-transit passengers will benefit by keeping a close watch for pickpockets in crowds.

Apartment Buildings

Beginning in the seventies, building codes required the installation of fire and smoke alarms in most urban multifamily dwellings. It became a practical, cost-effective possibility when technology made small units available for $10 or less. Likewise, security technology makes it practical nowadays for wireless or hard-wired intercoms to be required in all old buildings as well as new construction.

It came as a surprise to me that most of the experts I consulted consider that a voice intercom is more reliable than closed-circuit television scanners at doors and lobby entrances. Depending on the circumstances, an apartment dweller might be better protected by waiting to hear a familiar voice than by trusting a fuzzy television image that appears on a monitor that is flashing, popping, and usually out of adjustment.

Don Wagner of Electronic Entry Systems prefers the Marlee Company products that have an option whereby the apartment dweller can wear a small pendant. One coded push on the pendant will bring a paramedic, the superintendent, or an employee from a security monitoring firm on the run.

Some brand names that pop up most often among the specialists in this type of security installation are AIPhone®, Bogen®, and Talk-a-Phone®. These systems enable an intercom panel to be installed outside the building. Depending on a variety of options available, a push of a button will enable a visitor to contact any apartment dweller inside. The visitor will be admitted only after proper identification, by energizing the electric latch release on the main entry.

Hellman thinks the best system of all is to arrange with a private company or the Bell Telephone Company to install a regular telephone, the cost shared by all tenants. A visitor would dial the phone number of the person being visited. There are lock-out devices to prevent misuse of the exterior phone for, say, long-distance or toll calls. When used as a supplement to a routine intercom, it becomes a logical security device. The flaw of course is that the person being visited may already be talking to another person while the visitor stands in the street trying to cope with the busy signal. Again, technology is available to sound a "click, click" into an already busy line—at additional monthly cost, of course, but probably, all things considered, worth every penny of it.

Apartment dwellers also need to be concerned about previous tenants. My own preference is to personally change the apartment-door lock cylinder when I move into a new apartment. I might eventually provide the superintendent with a spare key which I've sealed in an envelope, thus eliminating his use of a passkey. Prior to that concession, I tell him he has my permission to break down my door, at my expense, if it is ever necessary to gain entrance.

I've used the technique in two apartments I occupied. The superintendents in both cases didn't like the idea at first, but when I explained it was a requirement of my job because of documents that were classified (well, to me, they were indeed secret), my system was accepted (with a hint of awe I might add).

Garages and Gathering Places

Increasingly, companies have taken on the card-key system of access. Many residential condominiums are supplying their occupants with card keys for the garage areas secured by rolling gates. Lounge areas within condos, hotels, and apartments are best secured by such devices and can be permanently coded to the original authorized holder. Card-key systems are available through all security installation companies. There are options that actually print out the comings and goings of all users, noting the time, number of entrants, weights of vehicles, and so forth.

Elevators

Unless I am absolutely sure of my territory I refuse to stay in any elevator with one other stranger, male or female. A petite young miss with a handgun is just as likely to ruin my day as a gorilla intent on beating me up for my wallet and credit cards.

I prefer crowded elevators or empty ones, wherein I stand near the panic switches. Many elevators will not stop at successive, intervening floors if I hold down the button for my own particular destination, although the operators are phasing out these older systems.

SPECIAL THINGS

Vacations

Surely you've read a dozen checklists of things to do when planning a trip. Cancel all deliveries. Arrange for routine maintenance while vacationing. Set up timers to do things like turning lights and radios off and on in a random sequence. Personally, I prefer leaving the air-conditioning equipment turned on. Burglars might be suspicious about the interior lights, but they retreat from a house attack if they hear the air conditioner turned on.

As I'll describe for you in a minute or two, in our community we're just getting a local neighborhood-watch program going. The doctor, wily fellow that he is, has come up with the idea of charging vacationing neighbors, who wish to pay, a dollar or two daily for special services such as adjusting the shades, watering the houseplants, feeding fish and birds, and generally inspecting the premises morning and night. He thinks it'll be a moneymaker for the organization, to offset the cost of sign maintenance, portable radio batteries, and such things.

It's difficult to imagine how anyone could not be aware of, or anxious to visit, the Eiffel Tower in Paris. I know, in my own case, I was virtually athrob with excitement the first time I found myself approaching this incredible monument in the heart of an enchanting city. And the very first object that caught my eye as I approached the elevator was a giant billboard with wording in letters at least a foot tall in virtually every language, stating Beware of Pickpockets. Protect Your Valuables.

All of a sudden the Eiffel Tower of my fantasies lost its golden glow and became little more than a rusty erector set. The thrill was gone. On those wretched days when business requires me to wear a three-piece suit I have no less than nineteen pockets in which to stuff articles of value. A topcoat and briefcase would provide several more hideaways to tempt me to carry attractions for every pickpocket.

Women are more limited in carrying-compartments. As we've noted already, women's costumes discourage security and self-defense. Is there any reasonably secure way that a woman can tote her currency, credit cards, cosmetics, valuables, and business materials around? The illustration on page 132 suggests one technique for reinforcing a briefcase. I've fitted out several, as shown, with an over-the-shoulder adjustable strap of the "folded-over" leather or plastic type of material. Our local hardware store sells a thin aircraft cable that can be threaded down the interior channel of the strap and then crimped over the connecting rings to the bag or case. The crimping is done with a special machine they have in their store. The cost of materials for an average bag might be 50 cents for the cable, 20 cents for each of two clamps, and $1 to swage them in place. For $2 the shoulder straps are strong enough to tow an automobile in an emergency.

The accompanying artwork demonstrates how I have reinforced a handbag for each of the several women associated with our clan. Radio Shack and other electronics stores sell a miniature buzzer that operates on a nine-volt battery. The buzzers screech at ear-splitting levels, particularly when they're bolted into a cleaned-up, painted-up cat-food can, which is then capped with a perforated plastic or metal lid and glued inside a handbag. A simple toggle switch is wired into the circuit and screwed into position near the handle of the bag. The buzzers retail between 50 cents and 90 cents. The batteries are free for the asking if you join Radio Shack's battery-of-the-month club.

The only problem we've encountered with this gadget is trying to explain it away on a couple of occasions at the security check-

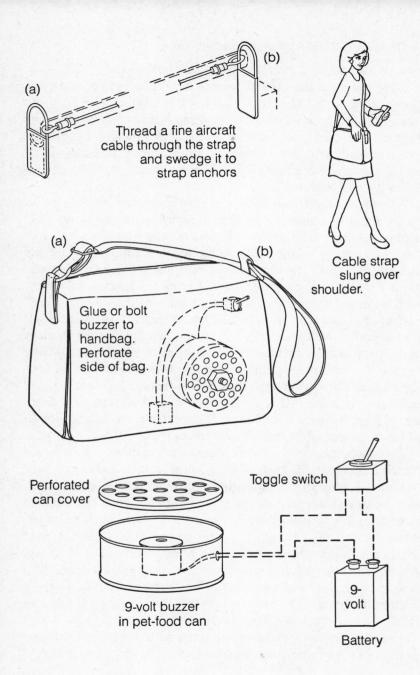

(a)

(b)

Thread a fine aircraft cable through the strap and swedge it to strap anchors

Cable strap slung over shoulder.

(a)

(b)

Glue or bolt buzzer to handbag. Perforate side of bag.

Perforated can cover

Toggle switch

9-volt buzzer in pet-food can

9-volt

Battery

out points in airports. One quick burst of the buzzer is enough to
have the attendants smile and send us on our way, safely, with all
possible speed.

Rape

Sadly, almost unbelievingly, we must face the horrid fact that a
million rapes are inflicted upon a million females each year. Police reports invariably footnote the speculation that likely there
are four or five times that number of rape incidents that go unre-
ported by women who are loath to discuss or report their awful
experiences.

Having read literally scores of suggestions about countering
rape, only two stick in my memory as the most practical for most
situations. They are unspeakable, disgusting things to read and I
will try to state them briefly, without embellishment.

1. A rape, unlike some murders, is usually a premeditated
crime. If an attacker is forcing a woman into position for rape,
she might force herself, somehow, to speak calmly, saying, "No,
not here. Over there. Nobody will see. I'll give you a blow job
you'll never forget." The attacker will almost certainly be so as-
tonished by this response that he will drop his guard as he drops
his pants, providing the woman a second or two to race, screaming, shrieking, clamoring for help. Experts assure me that this
technique has regularly proven to be effective.

2. The attacking man has two hands. One must hold his intended victim while he gropes with the other to expose his geni-
talia and tear at the woman's clothing. Now the woman must
concentrate all her energy to thrust her fingers, fingernails, even
her teeth, deep into his penis, twisting and tearing at the organ,
grabbing the testicles, twisting, squeezing, scratching to draw
blood and inflict utmost pain in the male's tender, private areas.
Then, she can run for her life, screaming, leaving her victim
writhing and wounded in pain, stricken by this unexpected and
personally customized counterattack.

I asked five police officers, three males, two females, if it is better for women to submit passively. All five said no.

10 *WHERE TO BUY, HOW TO BUY, AND WHAT TO CHOOSE*

Now you've got most of the basic things you'll ever need to secure and fortify your home, your business, and, most important, your own person and your loved ones. The last pages of the book, immediately ahead, will deal with the most important subject of all, the one for which you will need no equipment, only your own attitudes and the involvement of your neighbors in a Neighborhood Watch program. But first, of course, you must attend to your own needs.

YOU DECIDE TO DO IT YOURSELF

You either have now or can obtain readily enough wood and nails and screws and elementary tools to take care of things like your doors and windows. First things first. Do the basics to tighten up the house or the apartment. Then go after the garage and other outbuildings, if any. My next-door neighbor, the doctor, claims that from his reading of this manuscript and a review of Bruce Miyake's illustrations, he could personally add everything, from broomsticks to bolts, all homemade, on a Wednesday afternoon after a morning of golf. The doctor's wife declares he must be thinking about their son. She thinks the doctor would be fiddling around, trying to improve all of my recommendations, for at least six months.

Harry thinks that he could install the electrical and electronic things on a Sunday after building them on Saturday.

We all do these things differently, which is the whole idea behind this system of security—customizing! As I told you in the beginning, my own system is mostly cosmetic. I use the flashing LEDs, plastic tape around the windows, and I've just added the bike-chain links to the casement window. Also, to the systems already in the cars I substituted electric fuel pumps with hidden cutoff switches, as described on page 112.

They work splendidly, by the way, although they were noisy until I put rubber padding under them. This summer we're getting the BSR X-10 modules and I'll be able to control every electrical outlet, plug-in lamp, and appliance in the house from the fast-developing central command post near the headboard of the bed. Your department store will know about these systems.

BUT WHAT ABOUT THE ELECTRICAL COMPONENTS?

I contacted a sampling of the largest manufacturers of magnetic switches, light-emitting diodes, bells, and sirens. Do they welcome letters and phone calls from individual homeowners? Of course they do, particularly when they get compliments on their products. But as manufacturers they cannot take the time to advise one homeowner about one switch or one other small gizmo mentioned in this book. In fact, several of their senior executive officers observed that the law forbids them to sell their products one by one because of sales-tax regulations. They ship their products by the truckload to distributors and wholesalers, who distribute them to retail stores across the continent.

All of the items in this book that are factory-made can be obtained through Homemakers Desk, General Supply Electronics, 2202 Pico Boulevard, Santa Monica, CA 90405. Prepaid and credit-card orders (Visa, Mastercard) and established open accounts are shipped postage or UPS prepaid within twenty-four hours. Telephone orders are accepted between 9 A.M. and 5 P.M. Pacific time, and the charges for long distance are refunded on orders exceeding $50. Modest catalog sent free on request. Telephone (213) 450-5084.

DIRECT CONSULTATION

The principal consultant for *Crime Stoppers,* Jeff Hellman, will provide his best recommendations for any problems or questions you encounter if you outline them as briefly as possible in letters sent to him for personal attention, c/o P.O. Box 6421, Beverly Hills, CA 90212.

If you know exactly which system you wish to buy and would like additional data about the company that manufactures it, you might send your questions to the Better Business Bureau in your city or contact the municipal or county Bureau of Consumer Affairs or the comparable agency operated by your state government. None of these agencies will recommend any specific company or manufacturer of equipment, or monitoring patrol service, but they will tell you if there are any official complaints on the record concerning their products or services.

If you wish to get more data on specific organizations, you might contact the national trade association for many, though not all, of the manufacturers and distributors of alarm products and systems: Security Equipment Industry Association, 2665 30th Street, #111, Santa Monica, CA 90405; (213) 450-4141.

OTHER SOURCES

There's a likelihood that a municipal or county association of burglar and fire alarm companies is already organized in your community. Check through your telephone directory and Yellow Pages if you think such an organization might help you. I know of one young man who started his own security business after a few years of apprenticeship obtained by calling down the list of firms who held membership in the local association. These companies are looking for employees as well as customers. The push on security is getting serious. Jobs for security trainees are going begging.

For general, updated reading, there are monthly magazines directed at various levels of participants in the security industry. Check your newsstands and libraries. One of the giants in the publications of periodicals for security interests is Cahners Publishing Company (Division of Reed Holdings), Cahners Plaza, 1350 Touhy Avenue, Box 5080, Des Plaines, IL 60018. Their subscription department will advise you of the various periodicals that might be of interest to you, do-it-yourselfer or otherwise.

If you decide to get into the business professionally, the best place to start is making contact with your local community college or, failing that, the largest, best-known, most readily recognizable name of monitoring services operating in your area.

One organization of unusual interest is currently training telephone installers to add security systems to their available skills, with a view to opening their own phone/alarm companies now that the AT&T deregulation is under way. Contact the Telephony Marketing Group, 16 Yates Street, Ft. Morgan, CO 80701. They have launched a correspondence school that includes training via visual and audio cassettes.

For general information beyond the scope of this book, write to the National Burglar and Fire Alarm Association, 1133 15th Street NW, Washington, DC 20005. Phone (202) 429-9440.

If you simply wish to continue reading about the subject, obtain a reader's catalog from Butterworth Publishers, 10 Tower Office Park, Woburn, MA 01801. Their sole interest is security-oriented books, ranging from elementary to superscholarly texts.

HOW CAN YOU BE CERTAIN OF INTEGRITY?

If you're planning to invest a thousand or more dollars in fire and burglar alarms and continue paying because of tie-ins to monitoring systems, you might first examine your state's licensing and regulation.

Are your installation companies state-licensed? Is a licensing law coming along? Or can anybody hang out a shingle and get into security?

There are no regulations preventing homeowners from buying and installing their own types of systems if they are nonlethal. There are local ordinances springing up everywhere to penalize false-alarmers. Check with the local police if you have any doubts. Your suppliers will be able to clue you in.

11

SECURITY AND SELF-CONFIDENCE

OUR CHECKLIST OF SECURITY ASSURANCE

It was the evening of Valentine's Day when the doctor, Harry, and I convened in Harry's workshop and went down, step by step, point by point, a small stack of "security checklists" that had been sent to me from assorted police centers across the country.

The local police department has given up on checklists to be left with homeowners because often the individual insists that he or she did all the things suggested on the list but nevertheless, there they were, months later, trying to cope with the fact that their home had just been scoured of everything valuable.

Here's the list that we assembled from all the submissions that we examined and rewrote. The doctor, Harry, and I are virtually unanimous on each and every one of the following items. Will you make it a fourth? Check for "yes."

1. We have emergency numbers pasted on all our phones. ____
2. All of our doors and windows open with ease. ____
3. The same doors and windows can be locked down tightly. ____
4. We can all dial "O" (Operator) in the dark. ____
5. We always check before opening an exterior door. ____
6. We have at least two locks on each outside door. ____
7. We have all practiced out loud screaming "Help!" and "Fire!" ____
8. We routinely refuse to admit unidentified people. ____

9. Our door and window locks are checked *monthly*.   _____

10. Our various alarm systems are tested *monthly*.   _____

11. We protect our keys and credit cards as if they were gold.   _____

12. We have ongoing plans to improve our home security.   _____

13. We are certain we can keep calm in an emergency.   _____

14. None of us could be traced through our key rings.   _____

15. In the period when we needed baby-sitters we never permitted the sitters to admit others without first getting our permission.   _____

16. If we were held up, we would say, "Help yourself."   _____

17. We never leave our homes unlocked. Never. *Never*.   _____

18. We have prearranged for help from neighbors if we ever have an emergency (and vice versa).   _____

19. Our various fire-escape routes have been worked out.   _____

20. Lights are routinely left on, mostly on timers.   _____

21. We maintain lists of all credit cards and other important and numbered documents—multiple copies, hidden away.   _____

22. We regularly pester our insurance companies to reduce premiums because of our alarm precautions.   _____

23. All of our cars are always locked at all times.   _____

24. The cars are all theft-resistant in customized ways.   _____

25. We never give data of a personal nature to anyone over the telephone.   _____

26. If any of us ever had an obscene phone call, we'd immediately hang up. If such calls persisted, we'd seek phone company/police aid.   _____

27. The women in our families list only their initials in directories.   _____

28. We routinely walk the route taken to school by the local children, watching for hazards.   _____

29. When we go on vacation we arrange to have the shades and lights changed regularly by a neighbor.   _____

30. Our cars are all equipped with flashlights, tool kits, flares, and emergency accessories.   _____

31. All three of us have occasionally been too drunk to drive. We are delighted to let someone else drive. One of us once partied himself into a ninety-mile cab fare! _____

32. None of us is fearful about walking at night, even in a trouble-prone area. But we move briskly. _____

33. We routinely reject handguns as being too dangerous to ourselves and loved ones. _____

34. We all share a profound respect for most police officers. _____

35. None of us, to our knowledge, has purchased stolen goods. We do not buy items from unknown street peddlers for that reason. _____

The three of us are currently being jostled a bit by volunteering in the organization of a local Neighborhood Watch. It's eating up more time than we thought it would. We do not make excuses and get upset about having to attend meetings with people who are utterly new to the subject of security. We sit quietly while various johnny-come-latelies nitpick over things that Harry, the doctor, and I could answer in a word. We think it is essential that everybody go through the same process of wading into the pool, step by step, no shortcuts.

We know that our kind of democracy will survive only as long as people wallow around in it, in person. So far as we know, nobody has ever drowned yet in the milk of human kindness.

If you already have a Neighborhood Watch in operation in your neighborhood, be thankful. We are now working with our local Crime Prevention Bureau to establish one, which will cover an area of almost a square mile. The doctor is a member of the steering committee.

Our neighborhood is divided into nine patrol zones, each approximately a quarter mile by one-half mile in size. A peculiar little geographic quirk requires special handling of a special area in our neighborhood. Each has a Zone Captain and Team that hopes to enlist able-bodied men and women to patrol twenty-four hours daily, always on the lookout for unusual activity of a suspicious or dangerous nature. Our first effort to work four shifts daily, each six hours long, proved difficult. Things are getting better now as we are shifting into four-hour patrols, sixteen hours daily. We hope to go twenty-four hours later on.

Neighbors walk with neighbors in groups of two or three, their preference. They carry two-way walkie-talkies to speak to the headquarters office, which is finally being settled into a storage room of a local church.

Communications can be transmitted only from patrol members to the central command post, which will relay the message to police headquarters if there is cause for formal investigation. Approximately a third of the adults and older teenagers in the area have agreed thus far to participate in the program in some manner. We are being very selective.

We receive instructions during two sessions conducted by police officers. Our Neighborhood Watch signs have arrived and the city crews install them, at least one for each block. We pay $70 each, installed. We have a fund-raising chairman, who so far hasn't had to raise a finger; the contributions for signs, paper, and basic equipment have been coming in faster than we have needs.

Another committee, chaired by a woman in her eighties, is polishing a revised Protection for Children program, whereby any child who might be frightened by a stranger while on the way to or from school will have a participating home in line of sight, a place to run to for assistance and protection.

We're cleaning up our neighborhood. I hope you'll take a comparable interest in yours. But first, please, get busy with your own personalized system of crime stoppers, okay?

GLOSSARY

ALARM. One of the four main components of a security system. It can be a bell, siren, dialer, or any other type of alerting device. Part or all of the annunciator.

ALARM CONDITION. Usually the "caution" light in some systems, the early-warning light that something unusual is happening.

ALARM DELAY. A device within a circuit allowing entry or exit without sounding the alarm for a preset period.

ALARM LOOP. Also, just plain *loop*. It's the specific or general outline of security coverage that cannot be broken or changed without sounding an alarm. Same as *perimeter loop*.

ALARM STATION. Usually a manually operated device somewhere within the alarm loop; for example, the silent button on a bank teller's desk or the gadget in the cash drawer that sounds an alarm if the bottom (last) bill is extracted. This is the same sort of thing as withdrawing a plastic tag from between the jaws of an electrically connected clothespin, right? (That would be called a trip device.)

ANNUNCIATOR. One of the four main components of any alarm system. It monitors changes and usually includes the alarm itself as well as a power supply and reset button.

AREA PROTECTION. Most often a reference to a sonic or photosensitive electric method of guarding a large space, not only its access points.

ARMATURE. The moving core or blade of a relay. Its movement usually propels another section of the relay to open or close electrical contacts.

ARMING DEVICE. The master switch that starts or stops alarm systems. One of the system's four main components.

AUTOMATIC RESET. A device for automatically resetting an alarm system after it has stopped ringing for a preset period.

BREAK. The opening of a contact, thus interrupting current flow. Often the term is used to denote a possible failure in the system; its meaning depends on the context.

BURGLAR PAD. Usually a screen or panel of fine wire that covers an exterior window, skylight, or door. Illegal entry or breakage causes the wire to tear apart and create an alarm.

CAPACITANCE ALARM. An ultrasensitive device, requiring skillful installation, that detects the approach or entry of some foreign object or human body into a field of electrical energy. It's so delicately balanced that any presence of an alien kind will initiate an alarm signal. This system is known as a proximity alarm in many parts of the country.

CENTRAL STATION. A specific place at which signals from alarm systems can be received by either wireless or telephone/telegraph connections. If there is no audible alarm at the protected location, it's called a silent alarm, but is readily seen and heard at the monitoring center. The round-the-clock operators will usually send their own guards after alerting the police of burglar activity, or the fire company if the system is set up to recognize fire codes.

CLOSED-CIRCUIT SYSTEM. An alarm system wherein each of the detectors is connected in series, like a chain. If any link is "opened," an alarm is sent out. Larger houses and companies usually have zoned systems, enabling the monitors to observe not only that something unusual is taking place but allowing them to isolate the general area in which it's happening.

CONTACT MICROPHONE. A microphone that attaches directly to a surface to detect vibrations—even actual conversations on the opposite side of a wall.

CONTROLLER. One of the four main components of any alarm system. The controller will always monitor the condition of the detectors in the alarm loop and cause the annunciator to sound its alarm if the need arises. The controller is usually an electronic device with provisions for attaching the burglar or fire detectors and adjusting their sensitivity or delays, if applicable. Occasionally the power supplies for the alarm loops will be applied through the controller, which is most often maintained in a locked metal box, its wiring beyond reach.

CROSSOVER. A specialized security term to describe a wire or other insulated conductor connecting one detector area to another. One example might be the spot where it's necessary to insulate real magnetic foil from touching an iron or steel frame when passing from one windowpane on to another.

DEFEAT. The frustration or squelching of any device that would otherwise cause an alarm to signal a fire or intrusion. A power failure would defeat a system if it did not have provisions for backup electric energy. As fast as systems are invented, burglars study ways to defeat them.

DETECTOR. Same as a sensor; one of the four main components of any alarm system. A device, usually electrical, often mechanical, that can react to any change in conditions. It may be sensitive to movement, heat, smoke, moisture, or even barometric pressure. If it's electrical in construction it can either close or open its contacts, totally or partway, and thus set some sort of signal into motion.

DOOR CORD. A short, insulated wire with connector blocks at each end enabling current to flow from a fixed point on, say, a doorframe to the foil connector on the movable door (or window).

DOOR SWITCH. Any key-operated electrical switch. Also known as a shunt switch in many areas.

DOOR TRIP. A switch that's activated by opening or closing a door.

DOPPLER. An apparent change in the frequency or tone of a sound that is reflected from a moving object, as when a passing train sounds its horn and the sound seems to lower in pitch as it speeds away. It's utilized in many motion detectors.

ENTRANCE DELAY. The time between actuating a sensor and the sound of the alarm from the annunciator, usually determined by an adjustment in the controller. The delay is used when the authorized-access switch is located within the area being protected by the alarm. It enables the owner of the alarm to reach the controller and disarm the system before the alarm sounds.

EXIT DELAY. It works as the reverse of the Entrance delay, above. If the controller is located in the protected area, the system can be turned on, but permits the person to leave the area and set the final sensor without causing an alarm, within a predetermined time, like thirty seconds. Then, watch out!

FAIL SAFE. A special feature of a system enabling it to send an audible or visible signal of trouble if some component malfunctions or loses power.

FIELD. The area of coverage provided by ultrasonic, photoelectric, infrared, or microwave systems.

FOX LOCK. A bar wedged between a floor plate and a doorknob.

HOT BURGLAR. A burglar who enjoys working in the same room as a victim who may be sleeping, enabling him to keep the mark (victim) under observation. Similar to a *cat burglar.*

HYPE. An artless, usually amateurish, but serious type of heist.

IC. Integrated circuit, part of an electronic burglar alarm.

INDICATOR LIGHT. Any sort of pilot lamp or light-emitting diode that glows when indicating the status of an alarm system.

INFRARED. Literally, it means beyond red. It's an invisible part of the light spectrum whose rays are longer than visible red light. Increasingly being used in alarm systems. Sometimes referred to as black light, which is more properly applied to the ultraviolet frequencies.

INTERIOR PERIMETER PROTECTION. A line of wired or wireless protection surrounding a specific area, including all points of exits and entry. Also known simply as a loop.

INTRUSION. Unauthorized entry.

IONIZATION SMOKE DETECTOR. This unit is built around a minute amount of radioactive material that ionizes the air which passes through its sensing chamber, making it conductive, allowing electrical current to flow through that air between two energized electrodes. If any smoke particles enter that ionization area they decrease the conductance of the air by attaching themselves to the ions, causing a reduction in their mobility. When the conductance factor falls below a predetermined level, the detector circuit sounds off.

JAMB SPREAD. The result of cranking open an auto-type jack within a doorframe until the door is sprung loose.

LACE. A screen of ultrafine wire that is fastened in place over a burglar-alarm control system. In turn the lace is protected by a panel, so that any attempt to reach in and disconnect the main alarm system will cause the whole assembly to sound full alarm.

LOCAL ALARM. Bells, sirens, or other annunciating devices that are not connected to a central monitoring service.

LOCK MOUNT. A recent device enabling the owners of expensive car stereos to carry their units indoors with them by simply unlocking the bracket.

LOIDING. From *celluloiding*—a thin card of plastic is forced between the door stop and frame to shim back a spring latch.

MAGNETIC SWITCH. Two or more reedlike strips are fused in a glass tube, and then perhaps molded into an attractive plastic shape. The strips are separated or forced into contact by their proximity to magnetic forces, usually permanent magnets mounted in matching molds. Brand new to the market is a bias magnetic switch. If any burglar attempts to defeat a bias-type magnetic switch by introducing a magnet of his own, the effect will be a reversal of polarity and a sounding of the alarm, no matter what the snooper tries to do.

MICROWAVE. Extremely-high-frequency radio waves that can be bounced precisely between sending and receiving devices. If anything interferes with their transmission, alarms will be activated.

MOTION SENSOR. A detector that reacts to the motion of an intruder. Also, the gadget that switches on a car alarm if the vehicle is moved without authorization.

MULTIPLEXING. A method of sending two or more electronic signals over the same wire or broadcast frequency simultaneously, none interfering with the others.

NORMALLY CLOSED. Designation of a switch or circuit that can carry a current until its integrity is interrupted. Usually denoted as N.C. in reference to a switch.

NORMALLY OPEN. Designation of a switch or circuit that cannot carry a current until any unconnected components are united. Usually denoted as N.O. in reference to a switch.

OMNIDIRECTIONAL FIELD. The invisible field of influence covered by the radiations from certain alarm devices. Same as *field* when referring to ultrasonic, infrared, or photoelectric alarm systems.

ON-OFF SWITCH. More officially, the arming device that arouses an alarm system from its deactivated condition. Usually considered a main component in any basic electronic alarm system.

PASSIVE INTRUSION SENSOR. A passive sensor in an intrusion alarm assembly. It detects any intruder within its range, whether it is built to sense sound, vibration, or motion through its infrared capabilities. The sensor itself will not emit any of the characteristics it is made to detect. In an ultrasonic alarm system the sensor will require several methods of sensitivity adjustment to preclude any responsiveness to ambient sounds and extraneous influences. Very technical. Very unstable, unless tuned with precision.

PERIMETER PROTECTION. A physical example would be a wall surrounding the area to be protected. In alarm systems it could be any electronic, physical, mechanical, optical, or sonic encirclement that would detect the entry or exit of individuals in the area.

PHOTOELECTRIC. It refers broadly to electricity or electrical signals triggered by light. They are often called electric eyes. A routine PE sensor can be made to count by adding its interruptions in a circuit. A modulated alarm system depends on the reception of a light signal that conforms to a predetermined pattern of modulation; otherwise it will sound or activate an alarm.

PHOTOELECTRIC SMOKE ALARM. A commonly used sensor in which covers retard light but permit smoke to enter a small chamber. The photosensitive cell inside the chamber is influenced only by the minute amount of light generated to strike it. Any smoke particles interfering with that light passage would scatter and diffuse the light, activating the alarm.

PIEZO. Designates crystalline or mechanical structures that react to pressure or movement in the transmission and transference of electricity. Briefly, it converts mechanical movement into electrical potential.

PLUNGER SWITCH. A switch that responds to the push of a button.

PORTABLE DURESS SENSOR. A sensor worn by individuals to send any emergency signal to a specified monitoring station within its range.

PRESSURE PAD. Switch hidden within or under a carpet, grass, or entry mat to send an electrical impulse to an alarm by way of its normally open switch.

PULL TRAP. An intrusion detector utilizing spring-loaded contacts, such as an electrified clothespin. Most often actuated by a string stretched across a walkway or entryway, arranged to tighten and pull away a piece of plastic or similar insulator, allowing the contacts to close and sound an alarm.

RADIO-FREQUENCY MOTION DETECTOR. A sensor that detects the motion of an intruder via a radio-frequency magnetic field. Ordinarily it would be sensitized by any modulation within the field resembling a Doppler effect. Most RF motion detectors are certified as field-disturbance sensors by the FCC, which assigns them to one or more of the following frequency bands: .915 GHz (L-Band), 2.45 GHz (S-Band), 5.8 GHz (X-Band), and 22.125 GHz (K-Band). Sometimes known as microwave motion-detector alarms. (*GH* stands for gigahertz, meaning a billion cycles [changes] per second.)

RELAY. An electrically operated switch. There are two types in alarm use: an electromagnetic coil surrounding a spring-retained armature, plus two or more switch contacts; and a solid-state relay using semiconductors, mostly silicon-controlled rectifiers (SCRs).

STRAIN-GAUGE ALARM. A sensor-controlled alarm that detects changes in weight moving across it. Frequently used in floors and staircases.

SUPERVISORY ALARM SYSTEMS. These assemblies monitor the passage and movement of patrol officers along established routes of inspection. They are also set up to monitor production lines, water pressures within pipes, temperatures within processes, and liquid levels within supply systems.

SUPERVISORY CIRCUIT. An extra circuit within an alarm system installed to check on the status of all the arming devices, controllers, annunciators, alarms, et cetera.

SURVEILLANCE. Scanning systems via closed-circuit television and other monitoring processes depending on sound, pressure, heat, light, weight, et cetera.

TAMPER TRAPS. Usually these are locks to prevent entry into controller compartments of alarm systems. It is not unusual for an expensive, sophisticated alarm system to be protected by a slender, almost imperceptible pin that retains an interlock in the enclosure boxes of electric/electronic circuitry. Move lid, pin pops out and alarm sounds.

UL LISTED. It means that a product or device has been tested and approved for general service by the Underwriters Laboratories. The manufacturer is permitted to use the UL label if the devices are used in a prescribed circumstance and set of conditions.

ULTRASONIC. Frequencies above the audible range, usually beyond 20,000 cycles per second.

UNDERDOME ALARM. Usually a bell in which the mechanism and wiring ports are beyond reach, up under the dome of the bell.

VIBRATION SENSOR. Most often a normally open switch that reacts when it is shaken or it senses unusual movement in the apparatus to which it has been attached. It is most often rigged to remain in a closed circuit position once it has been activated.

WINDOW FOIL SENSOR. It's a strip of metallic foil, usually ³⁄₁₆ inch wide, often self-adhesive, that is set decoratively around a window to form a continuous path for the alarm-circuit current. If the glass of the window is broken, the foil cracks, changing the circuit status, and sounding the alarm.

ZONES. Smaller areas within large expanses, each isolated by fire doors and/or security doors as well as system loops that enable monitors to determine readily any location where intrusion or fire/smoke problems may be developing.

INDEX